USDA

United States
Department of
Agriculture

Forest Service

Pacific Northwest
Research Station

General Technical Report
PNW-GTR-868

September 2012

Oregon's Forest Products Industry and Timber Harvest, 2008: Industry Trends and Impacts of the Great Recession Through 2010

Charles B. Gale, Charles E. Keegan III, Erik C. Berg,
Jean Daniels, Glenn A. Christensen, Colin B. Sorenson,
Todd A. Morgan, and Paul Polzin

Authors

Charles B. Gale is a research associate, **Charles E. Keegan III** is an emeritus researcher, **Erik C. Berg** is a research forester, **Colin B. Sorenson** is a research economist, **Todd A. Morgan** is director of Forest Industry Research, and **Paul Polzin** is emeritus director, Bureau of Business and Economic Research, The University of Montana, 32 Campus Drive, Missoula, MT 59812; **Jean Daniels** is a research forester and **Glenn A. Christensen** is a forester, U.S. Department of Agriculture, Forest Service, Pacific Northwest Research Station, Forestry Sciences Laboratory, 620 SW Main, Suite 400, Portland, OR 97205.

Cover photographs: Clockwise from top left; yarder and slide-boom de-limber, residue pile in active logging unit along Oregon coast range, mill residue stored for use at bioenergy plant, sawmill in operation, log loader and skyline yarder, and skyline carriage in active logging unit along Oregon coast range. Lower right photo by Todd Morgan and others by Eric Simmons, University of Montana Bureau of Business and Economic Research.

Abstract

Gale, Charles B.; Keegan, Charles E., III; Berg, Erik C.; Daniels, Jean; Christensen, Glenn A.; Sorenson, Colin B.; Morgan, Todd A.; Polzin, Paul. 2012. Oregon's forest products industry and timber harvest, 2008: industry trends and impacts of the Great Recession through 2010. Gen. Tech. Rep. PNW-GTR-868. Portland, OR: U.S. Department of Agriculture, Forest Service, Pacific Northwest Research Station. 55 p.

This report traces the flow of Oregon's 2008 timber harvest through the primary timber processing industry and provides a description of the structure, operation, and condition of Oregon's forest products industry as a whole. It is the second in a series of reports that update the status of the industry every 5 years. Based on a census conducted in 2009 and 2010, we provide detailed information about the industry in 2008, and discuss historical changes as well as more recent trends in harvest, production, and sales. To convey the severe market and economic conditions that existed in 2008, 2009, and 2010, we also provide updated information on the industry and its inputs and outputs through 2010.

Keywords: Oregon forest products industry, timber harvest, timber receipts, log flow, timber-processing capacity, lumber overrun, mill residue, employment.

Highlights

The decline in U.S. housing markets, the global financial crisis, and record-low housing starts dropped sales of Oregon forest products from over $9 billion in 2005 to $5 billion in 2010.

- In total, 221 forest products facilities were identified as operating in Oregon during 2008:
    - 116 lumber facilities.
    - 28 plywood and veneer plants.
    - 22 house log manufacturers.
    - 20 pulp and board facilities.
    - 15 chipping, bark product, fuel pellet, and energy plants.
    - 10 post, pole, piling, and utility pole manufacturers.
    - 10 log furniture, cedar product, export, and engineered wood product manufacturers.

- Total 2008 sales were just over $6 billion. The mill residue using pulp and reconstituted board sectors accounted for 50 percent of the total, with sales of just under $3.2 billion. The lumber sector accounted for almost 23 percent ($1.5 billion) of the total. Plywood and veneer sectors made up 18 percent of total sales, with receipts of slightly less than $1.2 billion.

- By the end of 2010, more than a dozen large mills and numerous small mills had closed permanently. Operations at most other facilities were curtailed in both 2009 and 2010. Timber processing capacity dropped from 5,142 million board feet (MMBF) in 2006 to 4,531 MMBF in 2010. Capacity utilization exceeds 80 percent in good markets; by 2010 utilization dropped just under 57 percent.

- The Oregon forest products industry employed about 51,000 workers and paid about $3.05 billion (2008 dollars) in labor income in 2008. The primary sector accounted for about 70 percent of these employees (35,000 workers) and the secondary sector employed the remaining 16,000 workers.

- With the drop-off in demand, marked by the decline in U.S. housing markets that began in 2006, the global financial crisis in 2008, and post-World War II record-low housing starts in 2009, the sales value of wood and paper products from Oregon producers fell sharply from over $9 billion in 2005 to just over $5 billion in 2010.

- Annual harvests from 2008 through 2010 were the lowest since the Great Depression, with 2.7 billion board feet harvested in 2009. Similarly, Oregon lumber production declined following the collapse of the U.S. housing industry; production dropped to 4.7 billion board feet lumber tally in 2008 and recorded volumes of only 3.8 billion board feet in 2009 and 4.0 billion in 2010 (WWPA 2010).

- Although Oregon's industry retains 85 percent of its prerecession (2006) capacity, just over half of that capacity was utilized in 2010—well below the long-term average. This low utilization rate suggests both the possibility of additional mill closures or the potential for ramping up to expand output rapidly when market conditions improve.
- Eighty-two percent of the 3.6 billion board feet Scribner of timber harvested from Oregon timberlands in 2008 came from private lands. The remaining 18 percent came from state lands (7 percent), national forests (6.7 percent), and Bureau of Land Management lands and other public sources (4.5 percent).
- During 2008, sawlogs accounted for 77 percent of Oregon's timber harvest, and veneer logs accounted for 17 percent. Chipped logs made up about 5 percent and other timber products accounted for the remaining 1 percent.
- In 2008, Douglas-fir (*Pseudotsuga menziesii* (Mirb.) Franco) was the predominant species harvested on all ownerships, followed by western hemlock (*Tsuga heterophylla* (Raf.) Sarg.) and true firs.
- While Oregon's timber harvest was over 3.6 billion board feet, Oregon timber processors received slightly more than 3.5 billion board feet of timber for processing in 2008.
- During 2008, Oregon was a net log exporter of 95 MMBF Scribner shipped to other states or internationally, with total log imports of 321 MMBF, and log exports of 416 MMBF.
- The average log size processed by Oregon sawmills ran counter to a long-term trend and actually increased from 2003 to 2008. Sixty-two percent of logs processed by sawmills had a small-end diameter of greater than 10 inches in 2008 versus 54 percent in 2003.
- About 69 percent of the residue from Oregon's lumber and plywood facilities was used as raw material by the pulp and paper and reconstituted board industries. The remaining 31 percent of residues was used as fuel (26 percent), other uses such as animal bedding and landscape material (5 percent), or was unutilized (less than 1 percent).

Contents

Introduction

This report details the composition, operation, and timber and wood fiber use by Oregon's primary forest products industry during 2008. It also examines historical trends and impacts of poor wood markets from 2008 through 2010, including (1) estimates of wood fiber use and flow from the forest harvest through primary manufacturing, (2) a historical perspective of how the forest products industry and timber use have changed over time, and (3) a description of how the forest products industry has affected Oregon's economy over time.

Operations in the forest products industry are influenced by many factors, most commonly and frequently by market conditions and timber availability. From a national perspective, all of 2008 was part of the official recent Great Recession, which ran from December 2007 through June 2009 (NBER 2010). Despite the official end of the recession in June 2009, that year brought the poorest new home and lumber markets since the Great Depression, with 2010 showing only modest improvement. Additionally, Oregon's wood-processing capacity had dropped precipitously in response to the substantial reduction of federal timber volume sold during the 1990s. With these extreme market and timber supply conditions as a backdrop, this report discusses both historical trends as well as impacts of the extended difficult market conditions on Oregon's forest products industry from 2008 through 2010.

This report addresses "primary forest products," i.e., wood products directly manufactured from timber. These include lumber, plywood, veneer, posts and poles, pilings and timbers, and cedar shakes and shingles as well as products made from chipping or grinding timber, and from the mill residue (e.g., bark, sawdust, and planer shavings) generated during production of primary wood products. Products from residue include pulp and paper, particleboard, medium-density fiberboard, decorative bark, fuel pellets, fireplace logs, and thermal and electrical energy. Secondary products (i.e., goods made from primary products) include window frames, doors, trusses, and furniture; however, they are not included in this report.

The foremost source of data for this report is a statewide census of Oregon's primary forest products industry and out-of-state mills that received timber from Oregon during calendar year 2008. Firms were identified through telephone directories, land management agency timber bidders lists, directories of the forest products industries (Ehinger 2009, 2011; Lockwood-Post 2008; Random Lengths 2010b), and the assistance of the Oregon Department of Forestry (ODF), Oregon Forest Industries Council, and the online Oregon Forest Industry Directory. Firms cooperating in the 2008 Oregon census, including exporters and out-of-state mills, processed the majority of Oregon's commercial timber harvest. Inventory data were provided

> **Despite the official end of the recession in June 2009, that year brought the poorest new home and lumber markets since the Great Depression, with 2010 showing only modest improvement.**

by the U.S. Department of Agriculture (USDA) Forest Service, Pacific Northwest (PNW) Research Station Forest Inventory and Analysis (FIA) program (USDA FS 2011).

This census of Oregon timber processors is a cooperative effort between the University of Montana's Bureau of Business and Economic Research (BBER) and the FIA program within the PNW and Rocky Mountain Research Stations. The BBER, in cooperation with FIA analysts in the two research stations, developed the Forest Industries Data Collection System (FIDACS) to collect, compile, and make available state- and county-level information on the forest products industry in the West. The FIDACS is based on a census of primary forest product manufacturers located in a given state every 5 years. Through a written questionnaire or phone interview, manufacturers provide the following information for each of their facilities:

- Plant production, capacity, and employment.
- Volume of raw material received by county and ownership of harvest.
- Species of timber received and live/dead proportions.
- Finished product volumes, types, sales value, and market locations.
- Utilization and marketing of processed wood residue.

This effort is the second application of the FIDACS in Oregon; the first was completed in 2003. Previous to FIDACS, the BBER and the Forest Service research stations have been conducting periodic censuses in the Rocky Mountain and Pacific Coast States for almost 40 years. Before that, surveys and censuses of Oregon's forest products industry were conducted periodically by the PNW Research Station and ODF since the 1960s. Information collected through FIDACS is stored at the BBER in Missoula, Montana. Additional information is available by request; however, individual firm-level data are confidential and will not be released.

In the application of the 2003 FIDACS census, mills accounting for well over 90 percent of the timber-processing activity and over 85 percent of total facilities in Oregon provided specific information on their operations. Owing primarily to the extremely poor market conditions in 2009, with a substantial number of facilities having closed or sharply curtailed their operations, a little over 70 percent of total facilities responded to the 2008 census, representing a little over 85 percent of timber-processing activity. Other data sources (APA 2009–2010; Ehinger 2009, 2011; ODF 2009, 2010; USDC CB 2009; WWPA 2010) were used to estimate attributes for firms that did not complete the survey, to substantiate 2008 census results, and to provide 2009 and 2010 information. Discussions with mill personnel, questionnaires from the 2003 FIDACS, and the sources referenced above were also used to make estimates for nonresponding firms. The authors believe that the profile presented here is an accurate representation of the activity of Oregon's primary wood products industry during 2008 at the state and regional level and in various sectors of the industry.

Historical Overview and Recent Market Impacts on Oregon's Forest Products Industry

This section focuses on historical trends, the relatively recent past, current conditions, and predicted trends through the next few years. For a more comprehensive treatment of the earlier years of Oregon's industry the authors recommend reports by Andrews and Kutara (2005), Brandt et al. (2006), and Miller (1982).

Oregon has been a leading producer of lumber and wood products in the United States since the early 20th century and continues to rank first among the states in softwood lumber and structural panel production. Timber harvest and forest products manufacturing increased substantially during and immediately following World War II. Harvest exceeded 9 billion board feet for several years in the 1950s and 1960s. With the exception of the recession of the early 1980s, harvest remained above 7 billion board feet annually throughout the 1980s (fig. 1). From the 1960s through the 1980s (after the early 1980s recession), production and capacity remained relatively stable. Over half of Oregon's timber harvest came from federal timberlands during this period (fig. 2).

Harvest levels on private and tribal lands are highly dependent on market conditions. On Oregon's public lands, changes in federal and state land management policy have significantly reduced Oregon's harvest levels and milling capacity. The USDA Forest Service, U.S. Department of the Interior (USDI) Bureau of Land Management (BLM), and ODF sold and harvested less than 1 billion board feet annually through most of the 1940s. A post-World War II housing boom spurred a jump in federal timber offerings to over 3 billion board feet annually by the 1950s and 1960s. From 1960 to the early 1990s, federal lands provided at least 40 percent of Oregon's total annual harvest. However, significant changes in federal land management policy contributed to a large decrease in timber offerings starting in the late 1980s (ODF 2011, Warren various years).

The federal government's shift away from timber harvesting began with the listing of the northern spotted owl (*Strix occidentalis caurina*) as a threatened species in 1990, the listing of the marbled murrelet (*Brachyramphus marmoratus*) in 1992, and the listings of various species of salmon (*Oncorhynchus* spp.), trout (*Salvelinus confluentus*), and steelhead (*Oncorhynchus mykiss*). Habitat requirements for these species resulted in large areas of forest land being excluded from harvest. Additional restrictions on operating in roadless areas, as well as adminis-

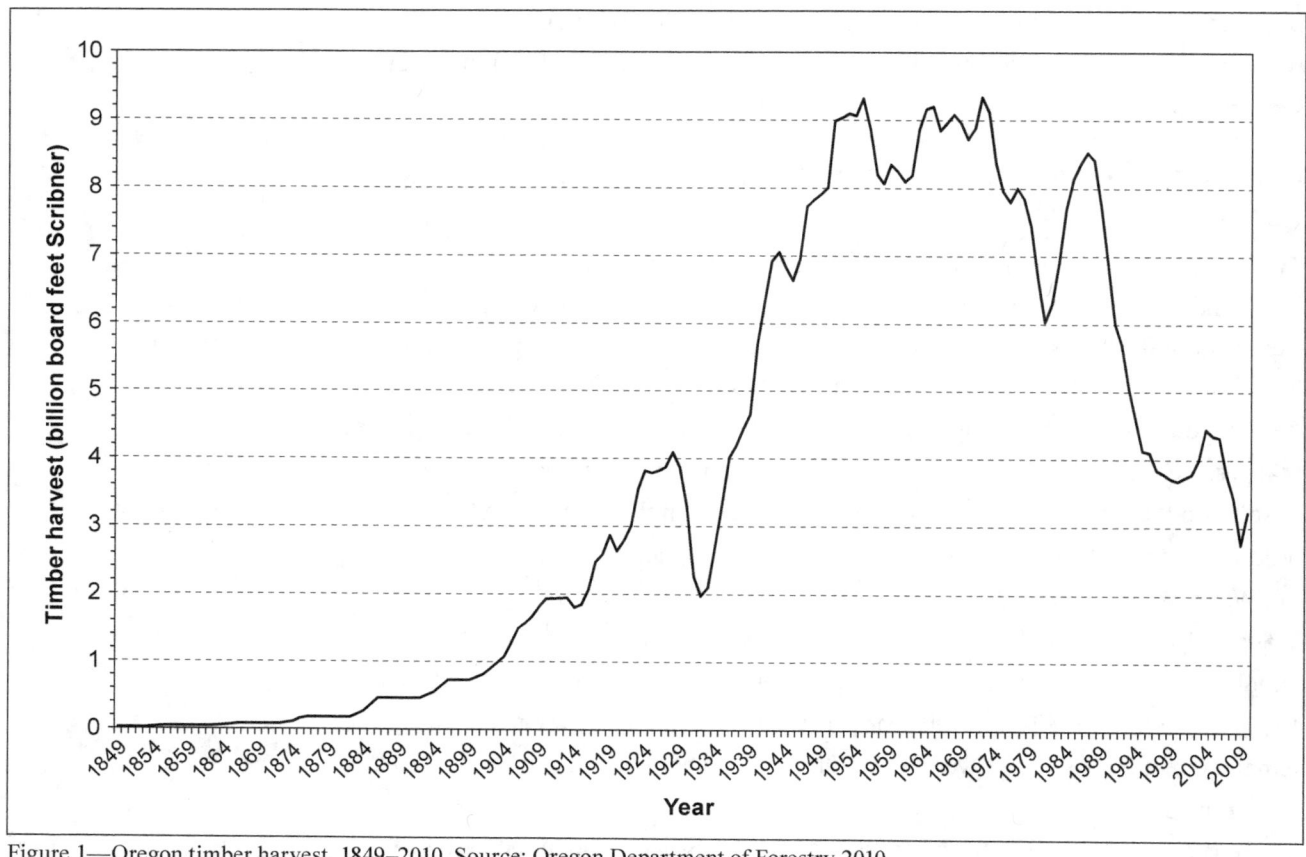

Figure 1—Oregon timber harvest, 1849–2010. Source: Oregon Department of Forestry 2010.

By 2008, over 74 percent of timber harvested in Oregon came from forest industry land. Today more than 80 percent of timber harvested in Oregon is coming from less than 40 percent of the state's nonreserved timber land.

trative appeals and litigation, contributed to further reductions in harvest levels by federal agencies. Between the late 1980s and 1999, federal timber harvest dropped by over 90 percent and harvest from other ownerships fell 20 percent (Brandt et al. 2006).

Harvest from state-owned lands has increased substantially during the past two decades, owing to a substantial inventory of commercial timber and high growth rates. Harvest from lands managed by the ODF went from approximately 140 million board feet (MMBF) Scribner annually during the 1990s to 341 MMBF in 2005, and averaged 270 MMBF annually from 2008 to 2010 (ODF 2011).

Ultimately, curtailed harvests from federal lands had a lasting impact on both timber harvest and wood products industries in Oregon. The proportion of timber harvested from public versus private sources in Oregon has shifted over time (fig. 2). By 2008, over 74 percent of timber harvested in Oregon came from forest industry land. Today more than 80 percent of timber harvested in Oregon is coming from less than 40 percent of the state's nonreserved timber land (fig. 3). Over the same

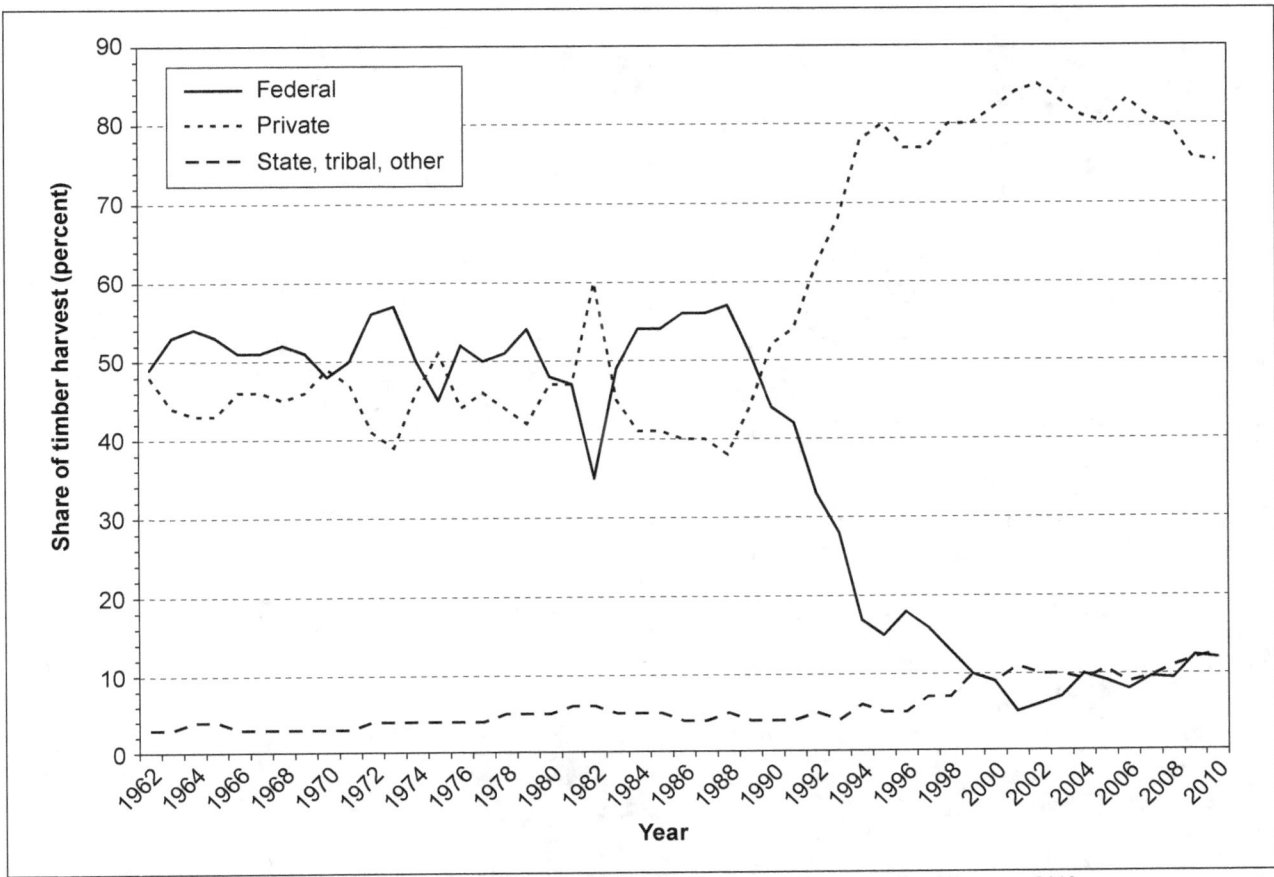

Figure 2—Changing shares of Oregon timber harvest, 1962–2010. Source: Oregon Department of Forestry 2010.

period, mill closures reduced Oregon's timber-processing capacity[1] by more than half, down from 9 billion board feet in the late 1980s to about 4 billion board feet by the late 1990s (p. 31). During this period when markets were generally good, lumber production from Oregon mills dropped by over 30 percent, and plywood production by nearly 50 percent.

The 21st century began with a relatively mild recession in 2001; conditions improved and product markets strengthened dramatically by mid-decade. Unprecedented demand for lumber and wood products resulted from growing demand for new housing; U.S. housing starts exceeded 2 million in both 2004 and 2005 (fig. 4). Oregon's remaining forest industry began to grow; timber-processing capacity rose

---

[1] Timber-processing capacity—The volume of timber reported in thousand board feet Scribner that could be processed given sufficient supplies of raw materials and firm market demand for products. This value was estimated for each facility by applying the product recovery ratios to production capacity.

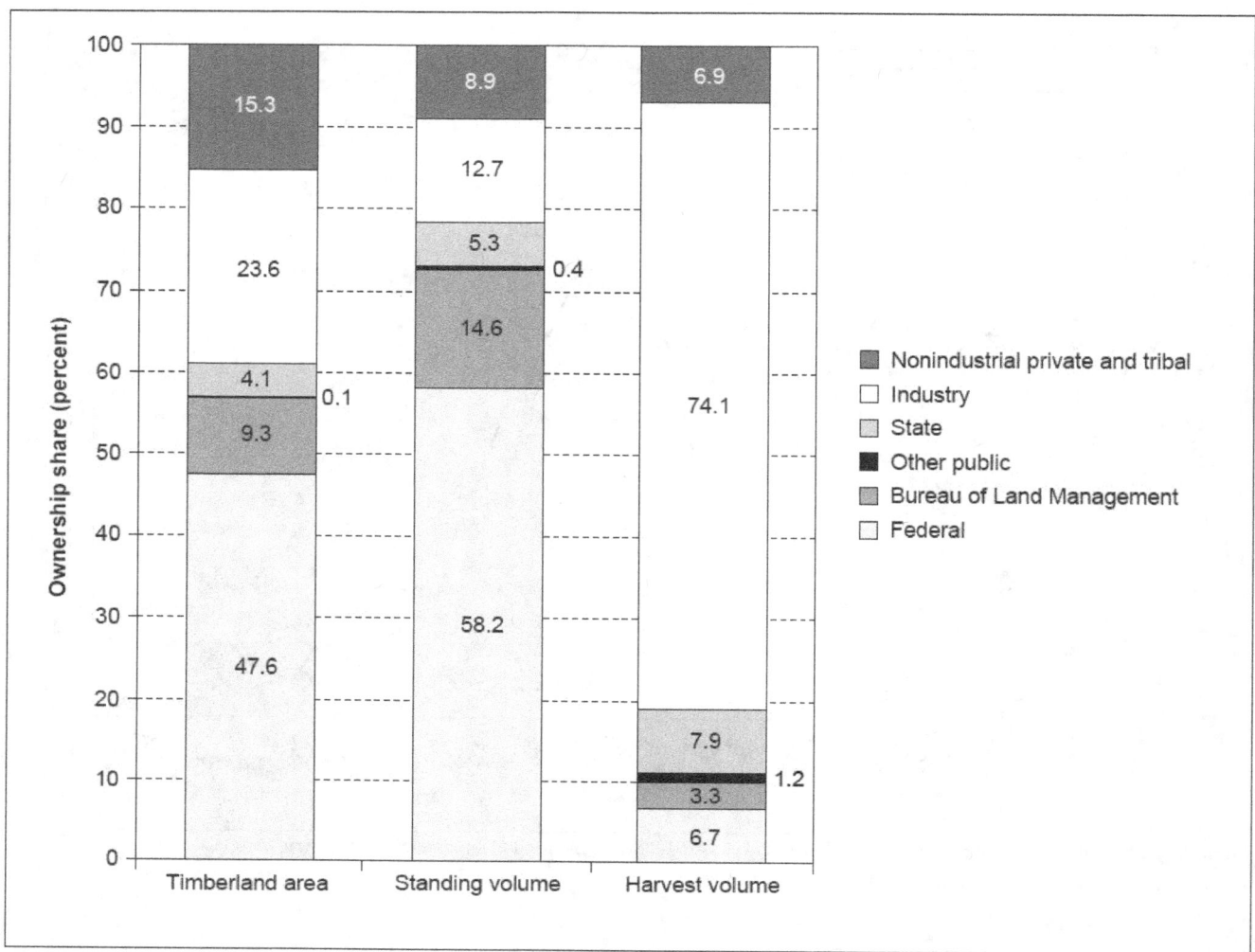

Figure 3—Characteristics of Oregon's nonreserved timberland by ownership class, 2008.

by more than 20 percent from lows in the late 1990s to 5.2 billion board feet Scribner in 2008. Lumber production rose from just over 5 to over 7 billion board feet over the same period (p. 31).

By 2006, the speculative housing price bubble that fueled the recovery of forest industries in Oregon became unsustainable. When combined with rising foreclosure rates as homebuyers defaulted on mortgage loans, the number of unoccupied houses in the U.S. housing industry began to rise. With increasingly large numbers of homes on the market, new housing construction fell; starts dropped from 1.49 million to 1.2 million units by 2007. The decline in housing starts was accompanied by a decline in home values and housing-related financial instruments, contributing ultimately to a massive global financial crisis in 2008 and 2009.

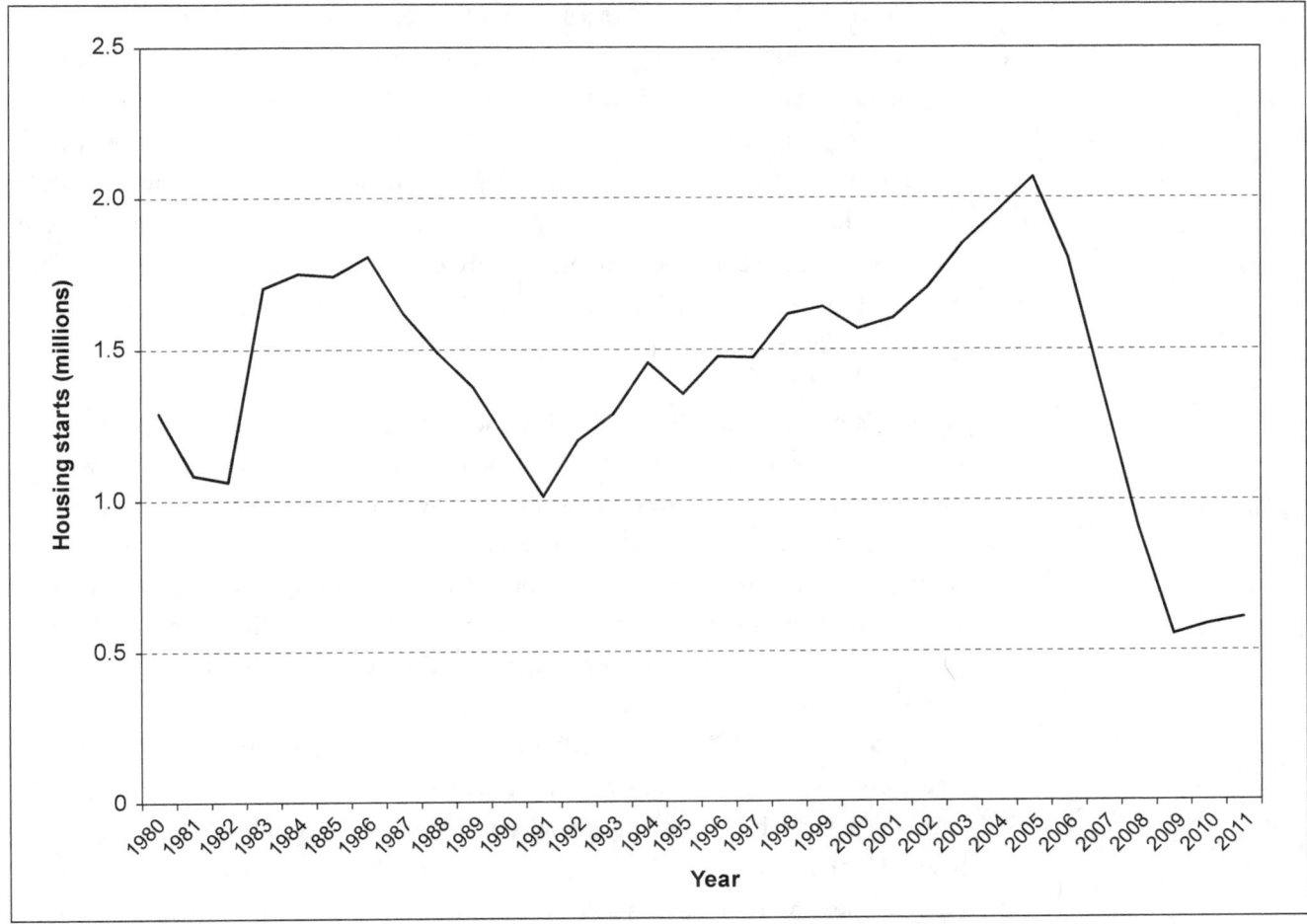

Figure 4—U.S. housing starts, 1980–2010. Source: U.S. Department of Commerce, Census Bureau.

The collapse of U.S. housing starts to 554,000 units in 2009 reduced lumber consumption in the United States to levels not seen since World War II. Lumber prices dropped about 40 percent from 2005 to 2009 while capacity utilization adjusted to new demand levels. Conditions improved only modestly during 2010. In response to curtailed production at mills throughout North America, rising log and lumber exports, and a slight uptick in housing starts, 2010 lumber prices were approximately 25 percent higher than the very low levels experienced in 2009. The expanding log export market of 2010 drove up log prices at a faster rate than lumber prices. Although a boon to forest landowners, high log prices negatively affected Oregon mills through rising raw material costs (Random Lengths 2010b; WWPA 2010).

The expanding log export market of 2010 drove up log prices at a faster rate than lumber prices. Although a boon to forest landowners, high log prices negatively affected Oregon mills through rising raw material costs.

The housing collapse and recession hit Oregon's forest industry hard. Harvests from 2008 through 2010 were the lowest three since the Great Depression, with 2.7 billion board feet in 2009, the lowest harvest since 1934. By the end of 2010, more than a dozen large mills and numerous small mills closed permanently from lack of demand. Timber-processing capacity dropped from 5,142 MMBF Scribner in 2006 to 4,417 MMBF Scribner in 2010. Lumber production dropped by half, falling from 7.4 billion board feet lumber tally in 2005 to 3.8 billion board feet in 2009, with just over 4 billion board feet of lumber produced in 2010 (WWPA 2010).

Future Outlook

As of this writing, there is little improvement in U.S. lumber and wood products markets although export markets and some pulp and paper markets have shown improvements. The improved export market has proved to be a mixed blessing for Oregon's industry, with higher log prices helping landowners but increasing costs for sawmills and other timber processors. Modest improvements are expected in domestic markets in 2012 with substantial improvements not likely until 2013 or beyond as U.S. home building recovers and global demand continues to increase (Random Lengths 2010a, 2011).

Although there has been a modest loss in timber-processing capacity in the last few years, Oregon's industry retains over 85 percent of its prerecession (2006) capacity. Just slightly over half of that capacity was utilized in 2010 versus a historic high of more than 80 percent during good markets. Low utilization suggests the possibility of additional mill closures or the potential for expanding output rapidly when market conditions improve.

Oregon's Timber Harvest, Products, and Flow

This section characterizes Oregon's timber harvest by land ownership, species, product type, geographic source, and flow to mills in Oregon and other states and countries. Several similar efforts analyzed Oregon's timber harvest in the past (Andrews and Kutara 2005; Brandt et al. 2006; Gebert et al. 2002; Howard 1984; Howard and Hiserote 1978; Howard and Ward 1988, 1991; Manock et al. 1970; Schuldt and Howard 1974; Ward 1995, 1997; Ward et al. 2000). These sources were used for historical comparisons for this 2008 report. Small differences may exist between the numbers published here and those in other sources owing to varying reporting units and conversion factors, rounding error, and scaling discrepancies among timber sellers and between sellers and buyers, and other reporting variations.

Oregon Timberlands

Oregon has approximately 61.4 million acres of land area, of which 30.1 million acres are classified as forest land.[2] Of this, about 24.5 million acres (81 percent) are classified as timberland,[3] 2.4 million acres are reserved[4] from timber harvest, and another 3.1 million acres are "available" other forest land. Of nonreserved timberland in Oregon, the forest industry owns nearly 5.8 million acres (24 percent), nonindustrial private forest (NIPF) landowners and tribal lands hold almost 3.8 million acres (15 percent), and public lands account for roughly 15 million acres (57 percent) (fig. 3). Approximately 14.1 million acres of forest land in Oregon are part of the National Forest System (NFS), and about 11.6 million acres (82 percent) of national forest land is nonreserved timberland (USDA FS 2011).

Ownership distribution of standing (i.e., live) timber volume differs slightly from land ownership. Total standing volume[5] on Oregon's nonreserved timberland is approximately 388.4 billion board feet Scribner log rule, including only trees greater than 9 inches d.b.h.[6] The majority, 225.9 billion board feet (58 percent) of the volume of trees greater than 9 inches d.b.h. is on NFS land, whereas 34.4 billion (9 percent) is on NIPF and tribal lands, 49.3 billion (13 percent) is located on industrial land, 20.4 billion (5 percent) on state land, 56.8 billion (15 percent) on BLM land, and the remaining 1.4 billion (<1 percent) on other public lands (table 1).

---

[2] Forest land—Land that is at least 10-percent stocked by forest trees of any size, or land formerly having such tree cover, and not currently developed for a nonforest use. The minimum area for classification as forest land is 1 acre. Roadside, streamside, and shelterbelt strips of timber must be at least 120 feet wide to qualify as forest land (USDA FS 2006).

[3] Timberland—Forest land that is producing or capable of producing >20 ft^3 per acre (1.4 m^3 per hectare) per year of wood at culmination of mean annual increment (MAI). Timberland excludes reserved forest lands (USDA FS 2006).

[4] Reserved forest land—Land permanently reserved from wood products utilization through statute or administrative designation. Examples include national forest wilderness areas and national parks and monuments (USDA FS 2006).

[5] Standing volume—Standing volume was calculated for all nonreserved timberland. Total aboveground stem volume, net of cull, was calculated on a cubic-foot basis for all trees larger than 5 inch diameter at breast height (d.b.h.). Scribner board-foot volume, net of cull, was calculated for all trees larger than 9 inches d.b h.

[6] Diameter at breast height (d.b h.)—Diameter of a tree stem, located at 4.5 ft (1.37 m) above the ground (breast height) on the uphill side of a tree. The point of diameter measurement may vary on abnormally formed trees (USDA FS 2006).

Table 1—Oregon timber harvest and standing volume by ownership, 2008

Ownership	Harvest		Standing[a]	
	Volume	Percentage of total	Volume	Percentage of total
	MMBF[b]	*Percent*	*MMBF[b]*	*Percent*
Industry	2,691.0	74.4	49,315	12.7
State	281.8	7.8	20,414	5.3
NIPF[c] and tribal	244.7	6.8	34,451	8.9
National forest	240.6	6.7	225,924	58.2
Bureau of Land Management	116.9	3.2	56,818	14.6
Other public	41.7	1.2	1,429	0.4
Total	3,616.8	100	388,351	100

[a] Indicates standing diameter at breast height > 9 inches on nonreserved timberland.
[b] MMBF = Volume in million board feet Scribner log rule.
[c] NIPF = nonindustrial private forest.

Harvest Levels and Harvest by Ownership

During 2008, slightly more than 3.6 billion board feet of timber was harvested from forests in Oregon, about 2.3 percent of average annual growth on nonreserved timberland[7] (Brandt et al. 2006), and sent to mills for processing. This volume was less than 1 percent of standing volume (table 1). Harvest fell to unprecedented lows the following year, when 2.5 billion board feet of timber was harvested in Oregon, rising somewhat in 2010 to 3.2 billion (ODF 2011).

Most (74 percent) of the timber harvested in Oregon in 2008 came from industrial timberlands (table 1). The remaining 26 percent came from state (7.8 percent), NIPF and tribal timberlands (6.9 percent), NFS lands (6.7 percent), and BLM and other public sources (4.5 percent). The 2008 NIPF and Tribal timber harvest was 4.6 percent lower than in 2003; these were the only ownerships to show a modest decline in harvest.

Harvests in 2009 and 2010 followed a similar trend. In 2010, over 75 percent of the harvest came from private and tribal lands, federal lands supplied about 11 percent, and state lands about 8 percent (ODF 2011). The proportion of harvest supplied by private and federal lands has remained relatively consistent since the large drop in federal harvest during the 1990s. State lands have become a more substantial contributor to Oregon's harvest in recent years (fig. 5).

The proportion of harvest supplied by private and federal lands has remained relatively consistent since the large drop in federal harvest during the 1990s. State lands have become a more substantial contributor to Oregon's harvest in recent years.

---

[7] Average annual growth on nonreserved timberland—Estimated from Forest Inventory and Analysis (FIA) plot measurements taken in Oregon during the 1990s (Brandt et al. 2006). The rate of average annual growth is not expected to change significantly from the 1990s to 2008; however, growth rates will be updated as soon as the estimate from FIA is available.

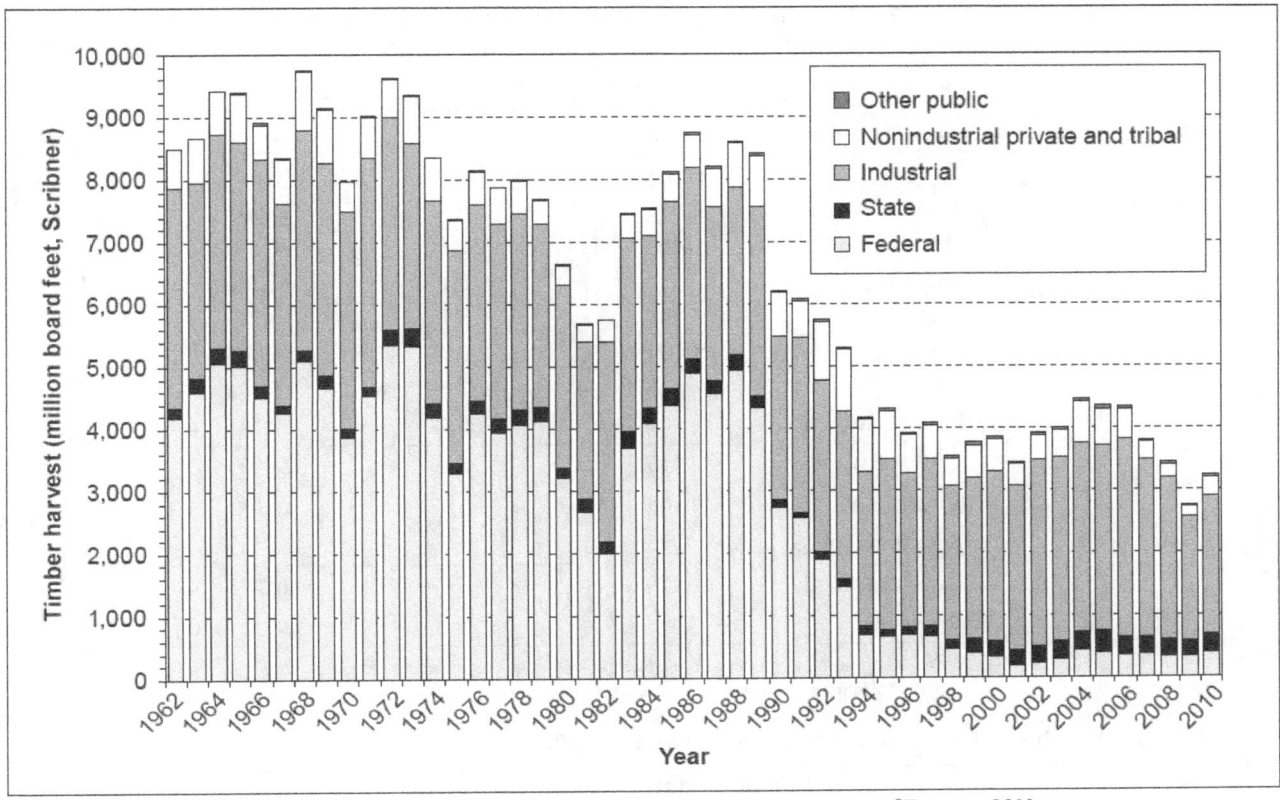

Figure 5—Oregon's timber harvest by ownership, 1962–2010. Source: Oregon Department of Forestry 2010.

Oregon's 2008 timber harvest was roughly 91 percent of the average annual harvest for the previous 10 years (1998–2008), but only 57 percent of the 40-year average. From 1993 to 2009, timber harvests from national forests in Oregon averaged 405 MMBF annually, accounting for only 10 percent of the state's total annual harvest. In contrast, between 1962 and 1992, NFS timber harvests in Oregon averaged 3,045 MMBF annually, 38 percent of the state's total annual harvest (ODF 2011).

Harvest by Species and Product Type

Softwoods accounted for 96 percent of Oregon's 2008 harvest; hardwoods made up the remaining 4 percent (table 2). Douglas-fir (*Pseudotsuga menziesii* (Mirb.) Franco) was the leading species harvested, accounting for 71 percent of total harvest. Western hemlock (*Tsuga heterophylla* (Raf.) Sarg.) followed with 13 percent, and other softwoods accounted for 13 percent. Hardwoods represented 3.6 percent of total harvest, with 2.9 percent red alder (*Alnus rubra* (Bong.) and 1 percent other hardwoods. During 2008, Douglas-fir was the major species harvested on all ownerships followed by western hemlock and true firs (table 3).

Table 2—Oregon timber harvest and standing volume by species, 2008

Species	Harvest		Standing[a]	
	Volume	Percentage of total	Volume	Percentage of total
	MMBF[b]	*Percent*	*MMBF[b]*	*Percent*
Douglas-fir	2,548.7	70.5	227,042	58.5
Hemlock	463.3	12.8	30,316	7.8
True firs	185.3	5.1	41,316	10.6
Pines	148.9	4.1	50,213	12.9
Spruce	71.4	2.0	6,343	1.6
Cedar	53.8	1.5	9,160	2.4
Other softwoods	15.8	0.4	9,543	2.5
All softwoods	3,487.2	96.4	373,933	96.3
Red alder	104.5	2.9	10,981	2.8
Other hardwoods	25.1	0.7	3,437	0.9
All hardwoods	129.6	3.6	14,418	3.7
All species	3,616.8	100	388,351	100

[a] Indicates standing diameter at breast height > 9 inches on nonreserved timberland.
[b] MMBF = Volume in million board feet Scribner log rule.

Table 3—Oregon timber harvest by species and ownership, 2008

Species	Industry	State	Nonindustrial private and tribal	National forest	Bureau of Land Management	Other public	Total
			Million board feet, Scribner				
Softwoods:							
Douglas-fir	1,884.1	224.8	164.2	149.5	100.3	25.9	2,548.7
Hemlock	369.3	42.6	23.5	9.8	5.9	12.2	463.3
True firs	121.3	8.2	21.5	25.4	6.8	2.1	185.3
Pines	77.2	3.0	16.9	47.9	2.4	1.4	148.9
Spruce	62.0	2.7	2.6	3.5	0.5	0.1	71.4
Cedar	48.4	0.0	3.7	0.9	0.7	—	53.8
Other softwoods	8.9	0.1	2.9	3.6	0.3	—	15.8
All softwoods	2,571.2	281.5	235.4	240.5	116.9	41.6	3,487.2
Hardwoods:							
Red alder	98.4	—	6.1	—	—	—	104.5
Other hardwoods	21.4	0.3	3.3	0.04	0.01	0.1	25.1
All hardwoods	119.8	0.3	9.4	0.04	0.01	0.1	129.6
All species	2,691.0	281.8	244.7	240.6	116.9	41.7	3,616.8

— = No value in cells.

Table 4 shows Oregon timber harvest by species over time with data compiled from previous industry censuses. Historically, Douglas-fir has been the leading species harvested (about 60 to 70 percent of annual harvest volume) in Oregon. The largest proportionate decline was in pine species. Although only about 4 percent

Table 4—Proportion of Oregon timber harvest by species in various years

Species	1968	1972	1982	1992	2003	2008
	Percentage of timber harvest					
Softwoods:						
Douglas-fir	65.1	61.1	59.2	61.2	65.6	70.5
Hemlock	10.6	13.4	11.5	9.9	8.8	12.8
True firs	5.9	5.1	5.2	8.9	8.9	5.1
Pines	13.6	14.5	17.7	14.0	6.6	4.1
Spruce	1.1	1.2	1.3	1.8	2.2	2.0
Cedar	2.2	2.0	2.1	1.5	2.0	1.5
Other softwoods	0.1	0.7	2.0	2.2	0.8	0.4
All softwoods	98.6	98.0	99.0	99.5	94.9	96.4
Hardwoods:						
Red alder	0.7	*a*	0.6	0.7	3.8	2.9
Other hardwoods	0.1	0.7	0.2	0.8	1.4	0.7
All hardwoods	0.8	0.7	0.8	1.5	5.2	3.6
All species	100	100	100	100	100	100

a Species not listed for given year.
Sources: Brandt et al. 2006, Howard 1984, Manock et al 1970, Schuldt and Howard 1974, Ward 1995.
Note: Percentages may vary owing to rounding.

of the harvest in 2008, pines accounted for almost 18 percent of harvest in 1982 and 14 percent of harvest in 1992. The decline is attributable to reduced harvest of ponderosa pine (*Pinus ponderosa* Douglas ex. Loud.) from federal forests in eastern Oregon (USDA FS 2012).

Four general categories of timber products are referred to throughout this report: sawlogs—timber sawn to produce lumber; veneer logs—timber sliced or peeled to make veneer for plywood or laminated veneer lumber; pulpwood/chipped logs—timber chipped or ground to use in pulp manufacturing or as fuel; and other timber products—timber used to manufacture cedar shakes and shingles, posts, small poles, utility poles, pilings, log homes, firewood, or log furniture.

During 2008, sawlogs accounted for 77 percent of Oregon's timber harvest and veneer logs accounted for 17 percent (table 5). Chipped logs made up about 5 percent and other timber products accounted for the remaining 1 percent. This distribution of timber harvest by product type paralleled findings from the 2003 Oregon mill survey reported in Brandt et al. (2006). However, table 6 shows that the proportion of sawlogs has grown while the proportion of veneer logs has declined over time.

Sawlogs have consistently been the leading timber product used by Oregon mills. Table 6 shows that the sawlog proportion of harvest remained relatively stable from 1968 to 1982 but began rising in 1992. By 2003, sawmills were consuming over 70 percent of Oregon's timber harvest. The veneer log component of harvest

The proportion of sawlogs has grown while the proportion of veneer logs has declined over time.

Table 5—Oregon timber harvest by product type, 2008

Product	Volume	Percentage of total
	Million board feet, Scribner	*Percent*
Sawlog	2,775.5	76.7
Plywood/veneer	617.4	17.1
Chipped logs[a]	196.5	5.4
Other timber products[b]	27.3	0.8
Total	3,616.8	100

[a] Chipped logs are primarily roundwood pulpwood and also include industrial fuelwood.
[b] Other timber products include cedar products, posts, small poles, pilings, utility poles, log homes, firewood, and log furniture.

Table 6—Proportion of Oregon timber harvest by product in various years

Product	1968[a]	1972[ab]	1982[ab]	1992[ab]	2003[cd]	2008[d]
	Percentage of consumption					
Sawlogs	61.1	58.9	57.2	67.3	72.9	76.7
Veneer	37.3	35	34.1	24.7	21.3	17.1
Chipped logs	—	—	—	—	4.4	5.4
Other timber products[e]	1.6	6.2	8.6	8	1.5	0.8
All products	100	100	100	100	100	100

— = No value in cells.
[a] Pulp and board included in "other timber products" for specified years.
[b] Log export included in "other timber products" for specified years.
[c] Log homes, firewood, and log furniture included in "other timber products."
[d] Displayed as harvest for specified years.
[e] Other timber products include cedar products, post, pole, piling, and utility poles.
Sources: Brandt et al. 2006, Howard 1984, Manock et al. 1970, Schuldt and Howard 1974, Ward 1995.

Closures and curtailments of sawmills reduce the availability of mill residue available to pulp and paper mills; therefore, those mills use more timber in round form to fill their fiber needs.

shows a different trend. In the late 1960s, the proportion of veneer logs was nearly 40 percent of total harvest owing to development and expansion of the plywood industry in Oregon. During the 1970s, Oregon's plywood industry began to decline, and, by 2008, the share of harvest going to veneer logs had fallen to 17.1 percent. This long-term decline was brought about by increased competition from oriented strand board producers, reduced volumes of veneer-quality timber on private lands, harvest reductions on federal lands, periodic increases in demand for veneer-quality timber for the export markets, and unfavorable economic conditions that depressed markets (Brandt et al. 2006). Other timber product uses have historically accounted for 5 to 10 percent of the timber harvested in Oregon with pulpwood/chipped logs being the largest component. The proportion of pulpwood/chipped logs tends to increase in years of weak lumber markets such as 1982 and 2008. Closures and curtailments of sawmills reduce the availability of mill residue available to pulp and paper mills; therefore, those pulp and paper mills use more timber in round form to fill their fiber needs.

Sawlogs and veneer logs were the leading products used in each ownership class. Table 7 shows that industrial private lands provided at least 70 percent of the total harvest for each product type. State timberlands were the second largest source of sawlogs and veneer logs followed by nonindustrial and tribal lands. Ninety-two percent of chipped logs and other timber products came from industrial lands.

Table 7—Oregon timber harvest by ownership class and product type, 2008

Ownership class	Sawlogs	Veneer logs	Chipped logs[a]	Other timber products[b]	All products
		Million board feet, Scribner			
Industrial	2,041.5	444.1	181.6	23.8	2,691.0
State	248.9	32.9	—	<0.1	281.8
Nonindustrial private and tribal	205.3	29.1	0	3.3	244.7
National forest	155.1	80.2	5.0	0.2	240.6
Bureau of Land Management	90.7	23.3	2.9	—	116.9
Other public	33.9	7.8	—	—	41.7
All owners	2,775.5	617.4	196.5	27.3	3,616.8

— = No value in cells.
[a] Chipped logs are primarily roundwood pulpwood and also include industrial fuelwood.
[b] Other timber products include logs for cedar products, posts, small poles, pilings, utility poles, log homes, and log furniture.

Douglas-fir was the species most harvested for sawlogs (77 percent), veneer logs (61 percent), and pulpwood/chipped logs (89 percent) (table 8). Cedars, primarily western red cedar (*Thuja plicata* Donn ex D. Don), accounted for 55 percent of the "other timber products" category.

Harvest by Geographic Resource Area

Oregon has traditionally been divided into two major wood-producing regions. The Western Region contains all counties lying west of the crest of the Cascade Range (fig. 6); the Eastern Region consists of all the remaining counties (Manock et al. 1970). Overall, the Western Region supplied 89 percent of Oregon's 2008 total timber harvest; the Eastern Region supplied the remaining 11 percent. This report expands this typology by splitting these two regions into four resource areas: the Northwest and Southwest Resource Areas in the Western Region and the Central and Blue Mountains Resource Areas in the Eastern Region (fig. 6), as indicated in table 9. In 2008, the majority of timber harvested in Oregon originated in the Northwest Resource Area. However, the Southwest Resource Area contained the greatest volume of standing timber.

Table 8—Oregon timber harvest by species and product type, 2008

Species	Sawlogs	Veneer logs	Chipped logs[a]	Other timber products[b]	All products
		Million board feet, Scribner			
Softwoods:					
Douglas-fir	2,056.6	374.1	107.2	10.9	2,548.7
Hemlock	337.2	80.8	45.3	0.1	463.3
True firs	106.3	75.1	4.0	—	185.3
Pines	113.3	34.6	—	0.9	148.9
Spruce	22.0	45.4	3.9	0.0	71.4
Cedar	37.2	1.6	—	15.0	53.8
Other softwoods	9.3	5.9	0.4	0.2	15.8
All softwoods	2,681.8	617.4	160.8	27.2	3,487.2
Hardwoods:					
Red alder	81.6	—	23.0	—	104.6
Other hardwoods	12.1	—	12.8	0.1	25.1
All hardwoods	93.7	—	35.8	0.1	129.7
All species	2,775.5	617.4	196.5	27.3	3,616.8

— = No value in cells.

[a] Chipped logs are primarily roundwood pulpwood and also include industrial fuelwood.

[b] Other timber products include logs for cedar products, posts, small poles, pilings, utility poles, log homes, and log furniture.

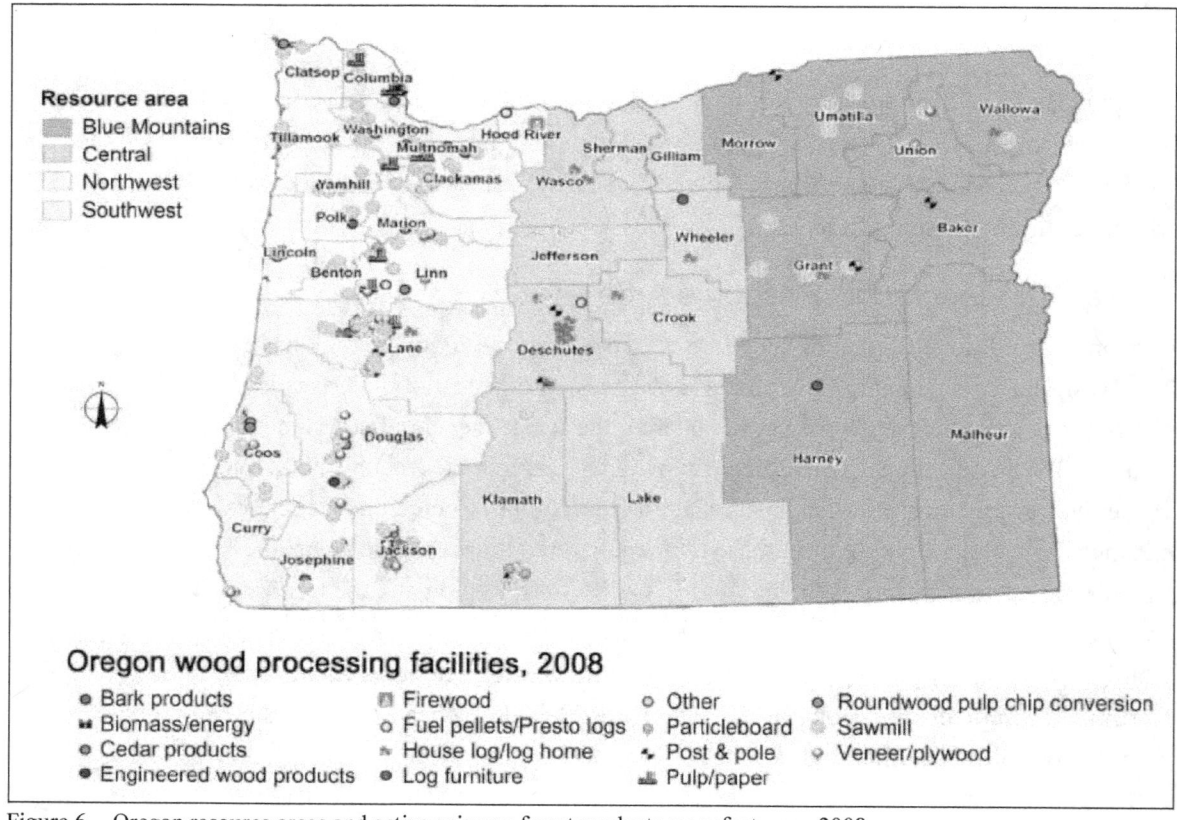

Figure 6—Oregon resource areas and active primary forest products manufacturers, 2008.

Figure 7 shows timber harvest by resource area from 1962 to 2010. The Northwest Resource Area provided approximately half of Oregon's total harvest in 2008, followed by the Southwest Resource Area, which supplied 35 to 40 percent (table 9). Prior to the mid-1990s, the Southwest Resource Area was the major timber producing region. Declines in eastern Oregon federal timber harvest resulted in substantial reductions in east-side volume delivered to Oregon mills over the past 20 years (Andrews and Kutara 2005)—this is particularly true for ponderosa pine. Although federal timber offerings have also declined west of the Cascades, accelerated harvesting from private and state-owned west-side lands partially compensated for shortfalls in federal timber supply. Eastern Oregon is different; there is relatively little privately held forest land to make up for reduced federal harvesting in the east. Overall, between 1962 and 2010, harvest levels fell by 62 percent, mostly owing to reduced harvesting in southwest Oregon.

Declines in eastern Oregon federal timber harvest resulted in substantial reductions in east-side volume delivered to Oregon mills over the past 20 years, particularly for ponderosa pine.

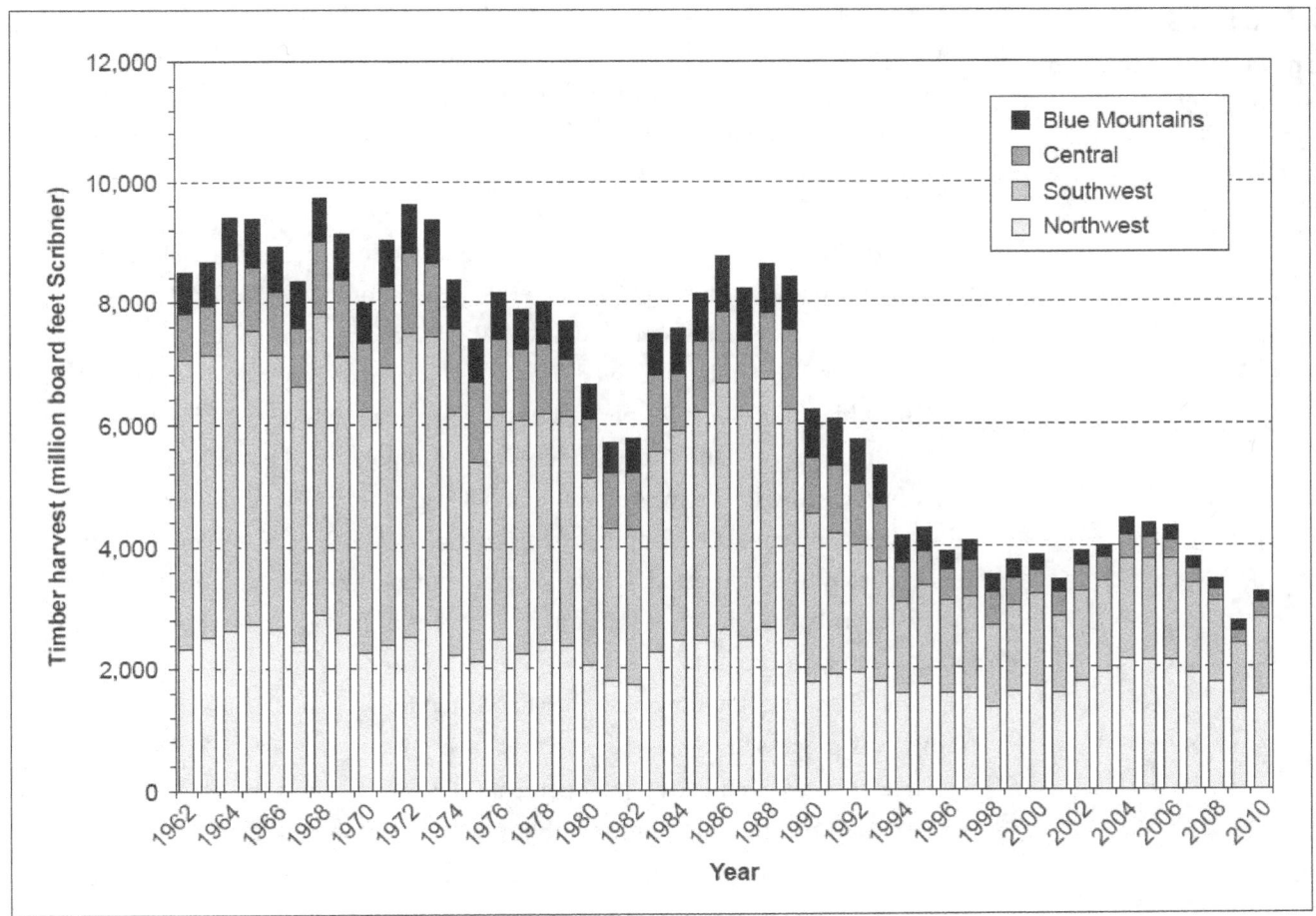

Figure 7—Oregon's timber harvest by resource area, 1962–2010. Source: Oregon Department of Forestry 2010.

Table 9—Oregon timber harvest and standing volume by resource area, 2008

Resource area	Harvest volume		Standing volume (>10 inches d.b.h.)	
	MMBF	*Percent*	*MMBF*	*Percent*
Northwest	1,865	51.6	112,892	29.1
Southwest	1,362	37.7	189,075	48.7
Central	208	5.8	47,736	12.3
Blue Mountains	182	5.0	38,648	10.0
State total	3,617	100	388,351	100

MMBF = million board feet Scribner log rule; d.b.h. = diameter at breast height.

Oregon timber processors received more than 3.5 billion board feet Scribner of timber for processing during 2008.

Table 10 lists the counties by supply areas and the volume of timber harvested from each county in 2008. In 2008, three counties—Clatsop, Lane, and Douglas—led the state with harvests of over 400 MMBF each. These counties are all in the Western Region with Lane and Douglas Counties in the Southwest and Clatsop County in the Northwest Resource Area. Within the Eastern Region, the proportion of harvest by resource area has been fairly consistent over time, with the Central Resource Area providing slightly more timber than the Blue Mountains Resource Area. Klamath, Union, and Wallowa are the major timber-producing counties in the Eastern Region.

Timber Flow

Oregon timber processors received more than 3.5 billion board feet Scribner of timber for processing during 2008. Over 90 percent of that volume was harvested from Oregon timberlands, consistent with the long-term dominance of in-state sources (table 11). Timber received from sources outside of Oregon totaled 321 MMBF, which represents 9.1 percent of the total volume processed in 2008. The marked increase of Idaho timber processed in Oregon was the result of major timber-processing losses in southern Idaho. Oregon timber was also exported to other states and countries for processing, and 416 MMBF (11.9 percent of harvest) was exported to Washington, California, and other countries for processing. More than 300 MMBF Scribner of Oregon timber went overseas, with the remainder to Oregon and California.

Table 12 shows the flow of timber harvested in Oregon. The majority of Oregon timber was processed in the resource area where it was harvested. Mills in each resource area received between 67 percent (Blue Mountains) and 88 percent (Northwest) of their timber supply from within their own resource area (table 12).

The Northwest and Southwest Resource Areas each received 39 percent of the timber volume coming from out-of-state. The Central Resource Area received about 5 percent (15 MMBF), and the Blue Mountains Resource Area received 17 percent (54 MMBF) of the out-of-state timber processed in Oregon during 2008.

Table 10—Oregon timber harvest by resource area and county, 2008

Resource area	Harvest volume	Percentage of total
	MMBF[a]	*Percent*
Northwest:		
Benton[b]	113.0	3.1
Clackamas	111.9	3.1
Clatsop	441.1	12.2
Columbia	137.7	3.8
Hood River[c]	29.0	0.8
Lincoln[b]	159.3	4.4
Linn[b]	268.2	7.4
Marion	53.1	1.5
Multnomah	12.7	0.4
Polk	129.6	3.6
Tillamook	201.5	5.6
Washington	120.8	3.3
Yamhill	87.2	2.4
Total	1,865.1	51.6
Southwest:		
Coos	303.5	8.4
Curry	79.8	2.2
Douglas	421.5	11.7
Jackson	92.3	2.6
Josephine	21.6	0.6
Lane[b]	443.2	12.3
Total	1,362.0	37.7
Central:[c]		
Crook	2.1	0.1
Deschutes	37.8	1.0
Gilliam	—	—
Jefferson	13.9	0.4
Klamath	76.4	2.1
Lake	30.2	0.8
Sherman	—	—
Wasco	42.6	1.2
Wheeler	5.0	0.1
Total	208.0	5.8
Blue Mountains:[c]		
Baker	14.7	0.4
Grant	17.9	0.5
Harney	15.9	0.4
Malheur	1.0	<.1
Morrow	1.1	<.1
Umatilla	14.8	0.4
Union	60.9	1.7
Wallowa	55.4	1.5
Total	181.7	5.0
State total	3,616.8	100.0

— = No value in cells.

[a] Volume in million board feet Scribner log rule.

[b] Previous Oregon forest products industry reports listed these counties in the west-central resource area.

[c] Counties use east-side scale.

Table 11—Log flows to timber processors in Oregon by state of origin

State of origin	1968	1972	1976	1982	1985	1988	1992	1994	1998	2003	2008
					Million board feet[a]						
Oregon	9,169	9,892	8,923	5,703	7,756	8,201	3,674	3,203	3,752	3,905	3,200
Washington	268	458	284	130	224	272	183	289	515	261	222
California	152	82	131	127	281	308	155	203	151	67	47
Idaho	c	1	1	0	11	16	17	47	18	58	42
Other[b]	5	0	1	0	0	1	4	33	64	8	10
Total	9,595	10,434	9,339	5,961	8,272	8,798	4,033	3,775	4,500	4,299	3,522

[a] Volume in million board feet Scribner log rule.
[b] "Other" contains log flows from states and countries not listed.
[c] For 1968 Idaho is combined with "other."
Sources: Howard 1984; Howard and Hiserote 1978; Howard and Ward 1991, 1988; Manock et al. 1970; Schuldt and Howard 1974; Ward 1995, 1997; Ward et al. 2000.

Table 12—Oregon timber flow by resource area, 2008

Destination	Geographic source of timber[a]				Out-of-state timber[b]	Total timber received in Oregon
	Northwest	Southwest	Central	Blue Mountains		
	Million board feet, Scribner					
Northwest	1,274.2	31.3	10.0	—	128.8	1,444.2
Southwest	196.1	1,320.7	57.6	0.6	123.4	1,698.4
Central	1.3	7.0	117.5	0.9	15.1	141.7
Blue Mountains	1.7	—	22.9	158.6	53.9	237.2
California	—	3.0	—	—	321.1	3,521.5
Washington and export	391.7	—	—	21.6		
Total Oregon timber harvest by resource area	1,865.1	1,362.0	208.0	181.7		3,616.8

— = No value in cells.
[a] See table 7 for counties in each resource area.
[b] Imports from California, Idaho, Montana, Washington, and international sources were combined to avoid disclosure.

Overall, Oregon was a net exporter of timber to other states or countries.

Overall, Oregon was a net exporter of timber to other states or countries (table 13). Over 90 percent of the 95 MMBF of timber flowing out of Oregon was in the form of sawlogs. Chipped/pulpwood, veneer logs, and other timber products made up the remaining 10 percent. Log flow into Oregon was primarily sawlogs and veneer logs (99.9 percent). Log exports were calculated using the Washington Mill Survey 2008 (2010), out of state mill questionnaires, export information from export facilities, and from "Production, Prices, Employment, and Trade in Northwest Forest Industries" (Warren, various years). Oregon exports for 2008 is the net balance of log flows into Oregon minus log flow out of Oregon.

Table 13—Oregon out-of-state timber flow, 2008

Timber products	Log flow into Oregon	Log flow out of Oregon[a]	Net in (net out)
	Million board feet, Scribner		
Sawlogs	250.5	(378.5)	(128.0)
Veneer logs	65.5	(5.0)	60.6
Chipped logs[b]	5.0	(31.0)	(26.0)
Other timber products[c]	0.1	(1.9)	(1.8)
All products	321.1	(416.3)	(95.2)

[a] Does not include logs received by Oregon export facilities for subsequent export to other countries.
[b] Chipped logs are primarily roundwood pulpwood and also include industrial fuelwood.
[c] Other timber products include logs for cedar products, posts, small poles, pilings, utility poles, log homes, and log furniture.

End Uses of Timber

This section traces the path of Oregon's harvested timber through the various primary processing sectors. Timber, primary wood products, and mill residues from manufacturing are commonly quantified in different units of measure. Timber inputs are generally reported in board feet Scribner west-side or east-side log rule. Volumes of mill outputs are provided in the measurement unit common to each product, such as board feet lumber tally or square feet of plywood 3/8-inch basis. Mill residue is commonly reported in bone-dry units (BDU) or bone-dry tons (BDT). In this section, volumes are expressed in cubic feet because expressing input, output, and residue volumes in a common unit of measure allows for more complete accounting of wood fiber through primary processing.

In this report, 1 BDU of residue is assumed to contain 96 cubic feet of wood, 1 thousand board feet (MBF) lumber tally is assumed to contain approximately 50 to 60 cubic feet of wood, and board-foot-Scribner-to-cubic conversions for timber vary by timber product type, which reflect log size and quality. See Keegan et al. (2010a, 2010b) for more detail on the conversions and relationships of timber, lumber, and mill residue volumes.

The following factors were used to convert board-foot Scribner log volume of the various timber products to cubic-foot volume (Keegan et al. 2010a):

- 4.35 board feet per cubic foot for sawlogs
- 4.48 board feet per cubic foot for veneer logs
- 2.41 board feet per cubic foot for chipped logs
- 4.45 board feet per cubic foot for other timber products

The following cubic volumes refer to Oregon's timber harvest and include timber products shipped to out-of-state mills; the figures do not include timber that was harvested in other states and processed in Oregon. Other manufacturers include producers of cedar products, log furniture, log homes, and house logs; these were combined to avoid disclosing proprietary information on individual firms. Figure 8 outlines timber flows by sector beginning with total statewide harvest and ending with finished primary products.

The 3.6 billion board feet of timber harvested in 2008 equates to 865 million cubic feet (MMCF) of wood fiber, excluding bark (fig. 8). Of this volume, 639 MMCF (74 percent) was delivered as sawlogs to sawmills; 138 MMCF (16 percent) were veneer logs shipped to veneer and plywood plants; 82 MMCF (9 percent) was chipped for pulp mills and board plants; and 6 MMCF (1 percent) were delivered as other timber products to various types of facilities (in fig. 8, see the first level of branching below total harvest).

Of the 639 MMCF of timber delivered to sawmills, 319 MMCF (50 percent) of bole volume became finished lumber or another sawn product, 298 MMCF (47 percent) became mill residue, and 22 MMCF (3 percent) was lost from shrinkage of green lumber. About 213 MMCF of sawmill residue was sold as raw material to manufacturers of pulp and paper, particleboard, medium-density fiberboard, and hardboard in Oregon and other states. About 69 MMCF of sawmill residue was used for energy; 30 percent of that residue was used by the sawmill producing it, and the remaining 70 percent was sold to other facilities generating electricity or other forms of energy. Residues used for miscellaneous other purposes such as livestock bedding accounted for 16 MMCF, and slightly less than 0.5 MMCF of sawmill residue was reported as unused.

Of the 138 MMCF of Oregon's timber harvest received by veneer plants in Oregon and other states, 79 MMCF (57 percent) of bole volume was processed into veneer, and 59 MMCF (43 percent) became residue. Of the 59 MMCF that became residue, 45 MMCF was sold as raw material to pulp and paper and board manufacturers. Approximately 3 MMCF of veneer mill residue was used for miscellaneous other purposes such as livestock bedding, and 11 MMCF was used for energy purposes.

About 82 MMCF (9 percent) of Oregon's timber harvest was in the form of pulpwood that was chipped and used to manufacture pulp, paper, or reconstituted board. These facilities received an additional 259 MMCF of mill residues from sawmills and plywood plants for use as raw material. In total, 341 MMCF of raw material was used for pulp, paper, and board products, and approximately one-quarter of that volume was from roundwood pulpwood.

Other manufacturers, including producers of cedar products, log furniture, and house logs and log homes, received 6 MMCF of Oregon's timber harvest. About 4 MMCF of this material became finished products, 1 MMCF of residue was used for

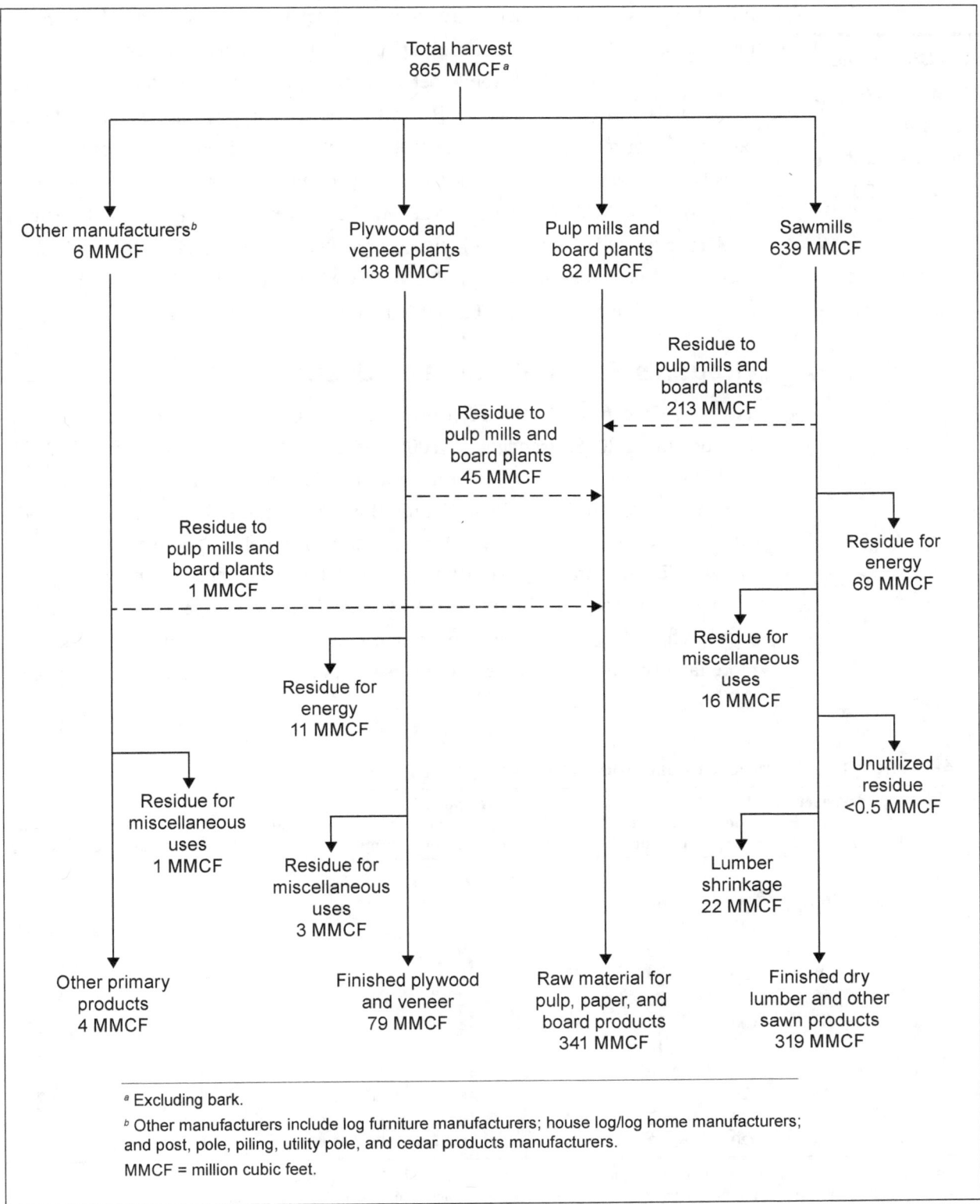

Figure 8—Oregon timber harvest and flow, 2008.

The FIDACS census identified 221 primary forest products facilities operating in Oregon during 2008.

miscellaneous purposes such as livestock bedding, and the remaining 1 MMCF of residue was sold as raw material to pulp, paper, and board manufacturers.

In total, 865 MMCF of wood fiber, excluding bark, was harvested from Oregon timberlands during 2008. About 341 MMCF was used as raw material to produce pulp, paper, or reconstituted board products such as particleboard or medium-density fiberboard; 319 MMCF became finished lumber; 79 MMCF became veneer or plywood; 80 MMCF was used to generate energy usually in the form of steam or electricity; 20 MMCF went to other uses such as animal bedding; 4 MMCF was used to produce other primary products; 22 MMCF was lost in shrinkage from green to dry lumber; and only 0.5 MMCF of wood fiber went unutilized.

Oregon's Forest Products Industry

The FIDACS census identified 221 primary forest products facilities operating in Oregon during 2008. Brandt et al. (2006) identified 249 facilities operating in 2003. Table 14 shows that the number of facilities has declined substantially over time, from 553 in 1968 to 200 in 1998. County Business Patterns (USDC CB 2011a) and other sources (Ehinger 2009, 2011) indicate that the number of active primary forest products facilities in Oregon during 2010 had fallen back to about 200.

The jump from 200 facilities in 1998 to 249 in 2003 is largely owing to differences in how data were gathered over time. The 2003 and 2008 surveys included more facility types than in previous years. Chipping plants were added in 1998 and

Table 14—Active Oregon primary forest products facilities by sector

Year	Lumber	Veneer and plywood	Pulp and board	Cedar products	Export	Posts, pole, pilings, and utility poles	Chipping	Log homes	Log furniture	Other facilities[a]	All sectors
				Number of active facilities							
1968	300	168	37	48	*b*	*b*	*b*	*b*	*b*	*b*	553
1972	262	133	40	43	38	10	*b*	*b*	*b*	*b*	526
1976	243	132	40	46	28	9	*b*	*b*	*b*	*b*	498
1982	161	101	36	34	32	8	*b*	*b*	*b*	*b*	372
1985	173	89	35	26	35	7	*b*	*b*	*b*	*b*	365
1988	165	87	33	24	33	18	*b*	*b*	*b*	*b*	360
1992	115	64	30	16	13	15	*b*	*b*	*b*	*b*	253[c]
1994	106	34	31	10	10	10	*b*	*b*	*b*	*b*	201[c]
1998	93	43	29	7	*b*	8	20	*b*	*b*	*b*	200[c]
2003	126	33	23	2	2	12	9	25	6	11	249
2008	116	28	20	2	*b*	10	8	22	4	11	221

[a] Other facilities include biomass/energy, bark products, engineered wood products, and fuel pellets/fire logs.
[b] Log export, posts, small poles, pilings, chipping, log homes, and log furniture were not included in the specified years.
[c] All the mills did not participate in the specified survey years.
Sources: Howard 1984; Howard and Hiserote 1978; Howard and Ward 1991, 1988; Manock et al. 1970; Schuldt and Howard 1974; Ward 1995, 1997; Ward et al. 2000.

log home, log furniture, bioenergy, decorative bark and mulch, and fuel pellets were included in 2003 and 2008. In addition, efforts to identify mills to include in the survey were expanded in 2003. It is possible that some mills were missed in earlier surveys. Thus, the downward trend in the number of active forest products facilities identified since 1968 has likely continued through the present time. Heightened efforts to perform a complete census of the industry in 2003 and 2008 likely resulted in the identification of a higher percentage and number of small mills than in the previous decade.

The downward trend in the number of active forest products facilities identified since 1968 has likely continued through the present time.

The decline in the number of mills in Oregon since the 1960s mirrors a similar trend prevalent throughout the Western United States (Keegan et al. 2006). Explanations for this trend include:

- Concentration of production into large, capital-intensive, more efficient mills.
- Lack of reliable timber supply following the reduction in timber sales from federally managed lands.
- Progressively smaller diameter timber available from harvest of second- or third-growth stands on private lands.
- The decline of cedar product facilities can be ascribed to the reduction in harvest of large-diameter cedar from old-growth stands. Cedar harvest currently is focused in second- or third-growth stands.
- Unfavorable market conditions that culminated with recessions in 1980 and 2007.
- Competition from such wood products as oriented strand board, which are not manufactured in Oregon and which compete with Oregon producers.

Factors affecting the structure and size of Oregon's industry are discussed in more detail in subsequent sections on the individual sectors and capacity.

Industry Concentrations

The majority (79 percent) of active forest products facilities were located in western Oregon (table 15). The Southwest Resource Area contained the largest proportion of lumber producers (44 percent) and plywood and veneer operations (71 percent). Lane County was home to the largest number of active forest products facilities in the state, with 33 mills operating during 2008. Douglas County followed with 22 mills. These findings are consistent with what previous surveys have reported (Brandt et al. 2006; Howard 1984; Howard and Hiserote 1978; Howard and Ward 1988, 1991; Manock et al. 1970; Schuldt and Howard 1974; Ward 1995, 1997; Ward et al. 2000). The Northwest Resource Area was home to 83 active facilities and the largest proportion of pulp and board plants (55 percent), chipping operations (75 percent), and other facilities (64 percent). Pulp and paper milling capacity was

Table 15—Active Oregon primary forest products manufacturing facilities by resource area, county, and product produced, 2008

Resource area/county	Lumber	Veneer and plywood	Pulp and board	Cedar products	Posts, pole, pilings, and utility poles	Chipping	Log homes	Log furniture	Other facilities[a]	All industries
					Number of facilities					
Northwest:										
Benton	4	—	—	—	—	—	—	—	—	4
Clackamas	9	—	2	1	—	—	2	—	1	15
Clatsop	2	—	—	—	—	1	—	—	—	3
Columbia	3	1	3	—	1	—	—	—	2	10
Hood River	1	—	—	—	—	—	—	—	2	3
Lincoln	1	—	1	—	—	1	—	—	—	3
Linn	5	4	3	—	—	1	1	—	1	15
Marion	2	—	—	—	—	1	—	—	—	3
Multnomah	2	—	—	—	—	—	1	—	—	3
Polk	3	—	—	—	—	—	—	—	1	4
Tillamook	3	—	—	—	—	—	—	—	—	3
Washington	5	—	1	—	—	1	—	1	—	8
Yamhill	6	1	1	—	—	1	—	—	—	9
Total	46	6	11	1	1	6	4	1	7	83
Southwest:										
Coos	11	1	—	—	—	2	—	—	—	14
Curry	1	1	—	—	—	—	—	—	—	2
Douglas	14	5	1	1	—	—	—	—	1	22
Jackson	3	6	2	—	—	—	2	—	1	14
Josephine	3	2	—	—	—	—	—	1	—	6
Lane	19	5	3	—	3	—	2	—	1	33
Total	51	20	6	1	3	2	4	1	3	91
Central:										
Crook	—	—	—	—	—	—	1	—	—	1
Deschutes	1	—	—	—	2	—	8	—	1	12
Gilliam	—	—	—	—	—	—	—	—	—	0
Jefferson	1	—	—	—	—	—	—	—	—	1
Klamath	5	1	2	—	1	—	—	—	—	9
Lake	1	—	—	—	—	—	—	—	—	1
Sherman	—	—	—	—	—	—	—	—	—	0
Wasco	—	—	—	—	—	—	2	—	—	2
Wheeler	—	—	—	—	—	—	1	1	—	2
Total	8	1	2	0	3	0	12	1	1	28
Blue Mountains:										
Baker	—	—	—	—	1	—	—	—	—	1
Grant	5	—	—	—	1	—	1	—	—	7
Harney	—	—	—	—	—	—	—	1	—	1
Malheur	—	—	—	—	—	—	—	—	—	0
Morrow	—	—	—	—	—	—	—	—	—	0
Umatilla	3	—	—	—	1	—	—	—	—	4
Union	2	1	1	—	—	—	—	—	—	4
Wallowa	1	—	—	—	—	—	1	—	—	2
Total	11	1	1	0	3	0	2	1	0	19
2008 total	116	28	20	2	10	8	22	4	11	221

— = No value in cells.

[a] Other facilities include biomass/energy, bark products, engineered wood products, and fuel pellets/fire logs.

concentrated in the Northwest Resource Area, which contained 80 percent of the pulp and paper plants.

The remaining 47 facilities (21 percent) were located in eastern Oregon. The Central Resource Area had 28 facilities and the Blue Mountains Resource Area had 19. Three board facilities were located in the Central and Blue Mountains Resource Areas combined. Deschutes County in the Central Resource Area had the majority of east-side mills with 22. The greatest proportion of house log manufacturers (55 percent) in Oregon was located in Deschutes County as well. Of the 19 mills in the Blue Mountains Area, the majority were lumber producers. Most of these mills were in Grant County.

Sales Value, Product Markets, and Market Areas

Oregon facilities reported the value of 2008 shipments of finished products and residues. Table 16 shows that product sales were led by pulp and paper followed by sawmills, plywood and veneer, and reconstituted board. These four industries represented 96.8 percent of total sales. The pulp and board sectors accounted for over half of all 2008 sales with just under $3.2 billion. The lumber sector accounted for almost $1.5 billion (24 percent) of the total. Plywood and veneer sectors generated 19 percent with nearly $1.2 billion in total sales. Other primary wood products sectors made up the remaining 3 percent of sales at $192 million (USDC CB 2009).

For the first time, the value of products from the pulp and paper ($2.8 billion) and reconstituted board industries ($375 million) accounted for over half of the total value of primary products at $3.2 billion. Pulp and board sales were greater than sales values reported by all other producers combined (USDC CB 2009, WWPA 2010). This suggests that the decline in housing starts affected lumber, plywood and

> **For the first time, the value of products from the pulp and paper ($2.8 billion) and reconstituted board industries ($375 million) accounted for over half of the total value of primary products at $3.2 billion.**

Table 16—Product sales[a] value of Oregon primary wood product sectors, 2008

Sector	2008 product sales
	Thousand U.S. dollars
Pulp and paper	2,821,171
Sawmills	1,461,155
Plywood and veneer plants	1,154,709
Reconstituted board	374,919
Other sectors[b]	136,748
Chipping facilities	41,369
Log homes plants	8,002
Posts, pole, pilings, and utility pole plants	5,217
Log furniture plants	860
Total	6,004,150

[a] Sales (free on board the producing mill).
[b] Other sectors includes bark products, cedar products, energy/biomass, engineered wood products, exports, and fuel pellet/fire log manufacturers.

other solid wood products producers disproportionately more than pulp and board industries.

Figure 9 shows the estimated value of sales of Oregon's primary wood processors for 2001 to 2009. Information collected about product sales value and destination in the 2008 survey was directly comparable to data gathered in the 2003 survey (Brandt et al. 2006). The remaining years were interpolated using annual data from the Annual Survey of Manufactures and periodic Census of Manufactures (USDC CB 2009). The sales value of Oregon's primary wood and paper products (free on board the producing mill) in 2001 was approximately $7.5 billion 2008 dollars. Strong demand for new housing resulted in strong markets for wood products; sales rose to nearly $10 billion in 2004 and remained over $9 billion in 2005. In 2006, conditions changed; U.S. housing starts began declining and fell to record-low levels in 2009. This collapse, combined with the financial crisis in 2008, led to sharp declines in the value of wood and paper products from Oregon producers to about $6 billion in 2008 and about $4.6 billion in 2009.

Table 17 reports the sales value and destination of Oregon's primary wood products and mill residues. Mills usually distribute their products either through

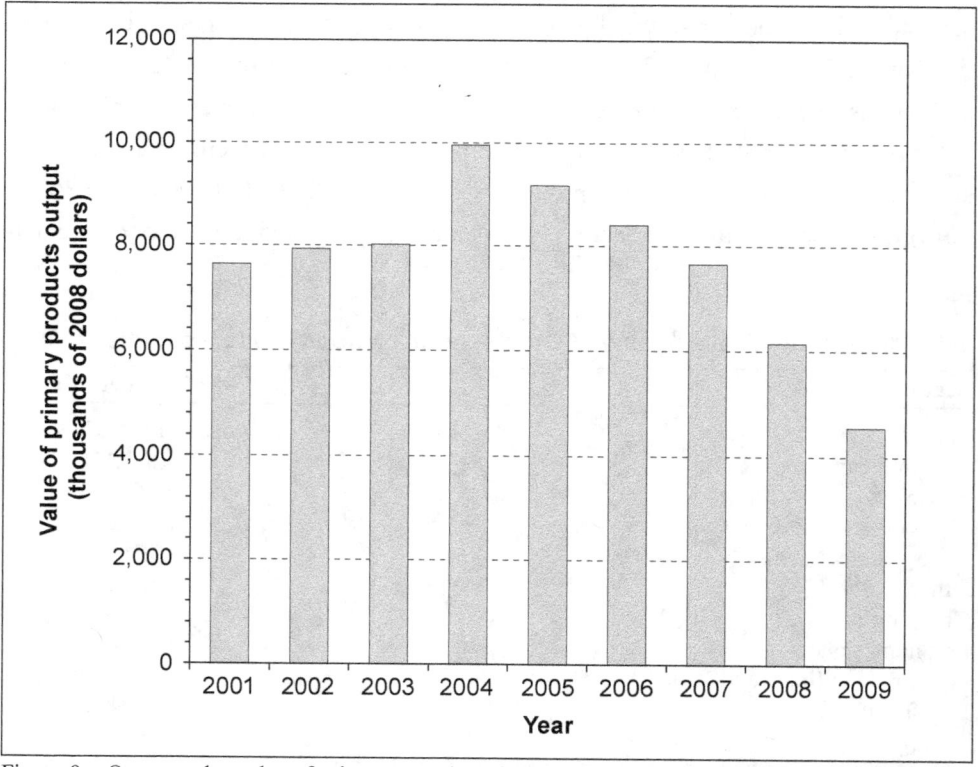

Figure 9—Oregon sales value of primary wood products output, 2001–2009. Source: Keegan 2010b, Brandt et al. 2006.

Table 17—Destination and sales value of Oregon primary wood products and mill residues, 2008

Product	Oregon	Far West[a]	Rocky Mountains[b]	North Central[c]	Northeast[d]	South[e]	Pacific Rim	Canada	Other[f]	Total
				Thousands of 2008 dollars						
Pulp and board[g]	216,313	2,324,183	292,909	143,282	21,708	48,135	97,811	35,592	16,157	3,196,090
Lumber	460,680	561,185	156,214	102,710	79,718	85,313	9,021	4,600	1,714	1,461,155
Plywood and veneer	466,486	303,697	77,604	124,456	105,380	60,053	564	16,469	—	1,154,709
Other primary wood products[h]	71,620	51,232	23,662	22,514	7,234	15,934	—	—	—	192,196
Total primary product	1,215,099	3,240,297	550,389	392,961	214,039	209,436	107,397	56,662	17,870	6,004,150
Residues[i]	230,766	55,381	—	—	—	—	—	—	—	286,147
Total sales value 2008	1,445,865	3,295,678	550,389	392,961	214,039	209,436	107,397	56,662	17,870	6,290,297
				Percent						
Percent total 2008	23	52	9	6	3	3	2	1	0	100
Percent total 2003	28	42	10	7	6	3	1	0	0	100
Total sales value in 2003 expressed in 2008 dollars	2,399,891	3,278,581	813,975	582,677	497,842	274,559	88,083	62,007	20,869	8,018,485

— = No value in cells.
[a] Far West includes Alaska, California, Hawaii, and Washington.
[b] Rocky Mountains include Arizona, Colorado, Idaho, Montana, Nevada, New Mexico, Utah, and Wyoming.
[c] North Central includes Illinois, Indiana, Iowa, Kansas, Michigan, Minnesota, Missouri, Nebraska, North Dakota, Ohio, South Dakota, and Wisconsin.
[d] Northeast includes Connecticut, Maine, Massachusetts, New Hampshire, New Jersey, New York, Pennsylvania, Rhode Island, and Vermont.
[e] South includes Alabama, Arkansas, Delaware, Florida, Georgia, Kentucky, Louisiana, Maryland, Mississippi, North Carolina, Oklahoma, South Carolina, Tennessee, Texas, Virginia, and West Virginia.
[f] Other includes Europe and Mexico.
[g] Pulp and board includes pulp, paper, reconstituted board, bark, wood pellets, and other energy products.
[h] Other primary wood products include cedar products, export logs, log furniture, house logs, posts, small poles, pilings, and utility poles.
[i] Mill residues in Far West include all out-of-state mill residue sales.

At \$3.3 billion, the Far West states comprised the largest market for Oregon's primary wood and paper products.

their own distribution channels or through independent wholesalers and selling agents. Because of subsequent downstream transactions, the geographic destination reported here may not precisely reflect the final delivery points of shipments.

At \$3.3 billion, the Far West states comprised the largest market for Oregon's primary wood and paper products; sales represented 52 percent of the total. The majority of these sales occurred in pulp and reconstituted board followed by the lumber sector. Plywood, veneer, and other primary products were mostly sold out of state; sales to Oregon buyers of primary products were \$1.4 billion overall. Many of the sales to Oregon buyers were sold again for further processing in other states.

Market destinations for Oregon products in 2008 are only modestly different from 2003 (Brandt et al. 2006). The share of sales in Oregon and other Far West states increased from 70 percent in 2003 to 75 percent in 2008 mostly owing to modest gains in sales to Far West states. Another difference between the two periods was in product exports, which rose from less than 1 percent in 2003 to 3 percent in 2008. Also, sales to the Northeast Region fell from 6 to 3 percent.

Trends and Capacity by Sector

This section discusses market trends and mill survey results by sector. Specifically, we examine productivity in the sawmill, plywood, pulp and board, and other primary products sectors.

Sawmill Sector

Figure 10 shows Oregon lumber production, which peaked in 1955 at just under 9.2 billion board feet lumber tally. Between 1955 and the late 1970s, lumber production gradually declined, with minor year-to-year troughs and peaks, to 7.3 billion in 1979. Production declined during this time primarily because timber volume was diverted to plywood manufacturing. Lumber production dropped substantially during the recession of the early 1980s to just under 4.7 billion lumber tally in 1982. Following the recession lumber markets improved and lumber production climbed consistently. The peak of 8.8 billion board feet in 1987 was just below the peak of the early 1950s.

The drop in federal harvest in the first half of the 1990s led to closures and a sizable drop in lumber output in Oregon to a low in 1995 of under 5 billion board feet (Keegan et al. 2006). In response, harvests from nonfederal lands rose. From the mid-1990s through the early 2000s, lumber production rose steadily to a peak of 7.4 billion board feet lumber tally in 2005. Following this period of strong markets, lumber production in Oregon declined drastically with the collapse of the U.S. housing industry. Production in 2008 dropped to 4.7 billion board feet lumber tally, then to 3.8 billion in 2009 and 4 billion in 2010 (WWPA 2010).

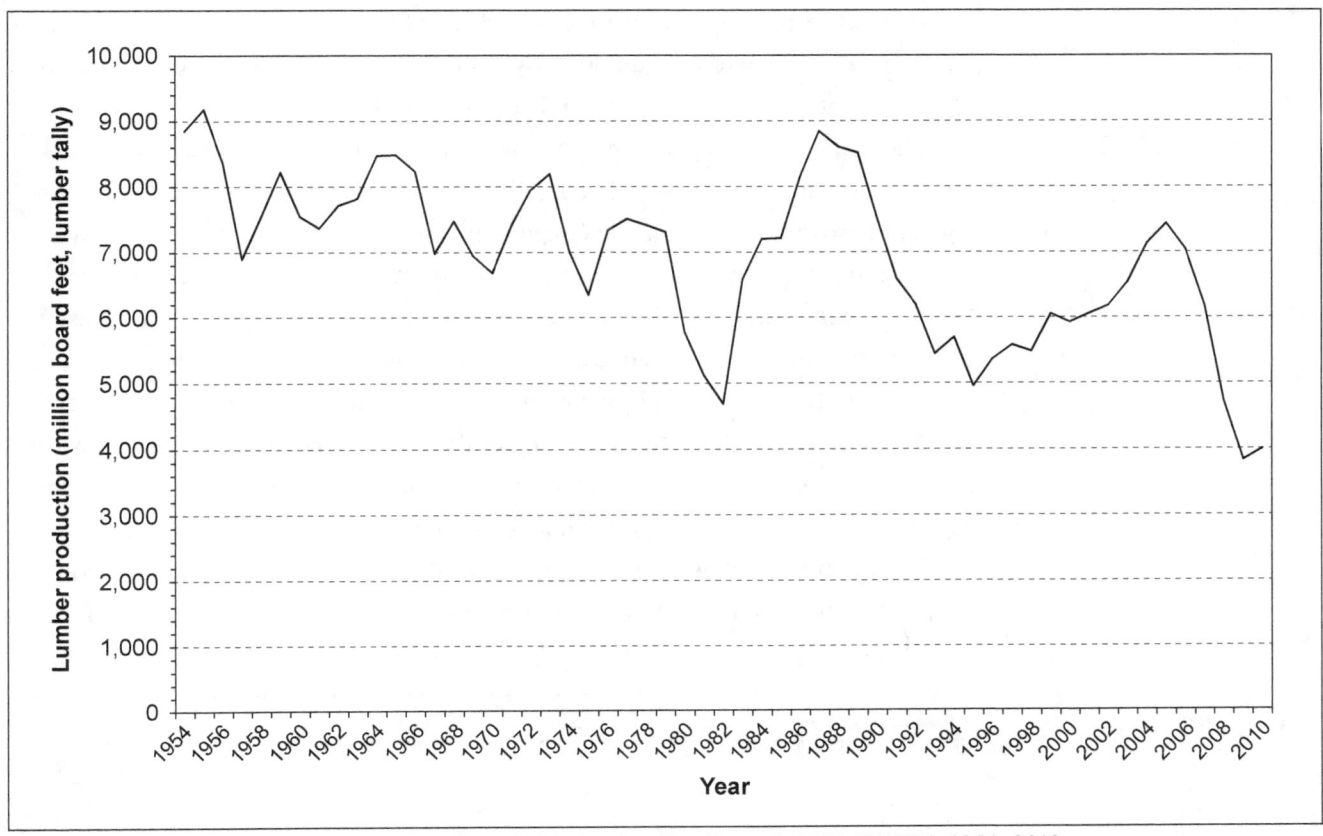

Figure 10—Oregon's lumber production, 1954–2009. Source: Brodie et al. 1978; WWPA 1954–2010.

Sawmill lumber recovery—

Product recovery ratios, or the volume of output per unit of input, are a measure of efficiency reported by Oregon's sawmills as lumber recovery factors (LRF) and overrun. The LRF is the lumber output (in thousand board feet lumber tally) divided by the timber input (thousand cubic feet). Lumber overrun (LO) is the amount of lumber actually recovered in excess of the volume predicted by the log scale, expressed as a percentage of the log scale (Keegan et al. 2010b). Although LO is the most commonly quoted measure of lumber recovery and mill efficiency, LO fails to accurately portray differences in lumber recovery, primarily owing to flaws in the Scribner log scale used to estimate timber volume. As log diameters decrease, generally the Scribner log rule used in Oregon increasingly underestimates the volume of lumber that can be recovered from a log, thus increasing overrun. The LRF measure better illustrates the relationship between rising lumber output and improvements in technology and sawing techniques (Keegan et al. 2010b).

Both LO and LRF have risen substantially over the past 40 years as shown in figure 11 and table 18. Lumber overrun increased from 1.27 in 1968 to 2.07 in 2003 (Brandt et al. 2006, Keegan et al. 2010b, Manock et al. 1970), before a slight decline to 2.04 in 2008 (fig. 11). Lumber recovery factor followed a similar pattern, increasing from about 7 board feet lumber tally per cubic foot of sawlog input in 1968 to 8.7 board feet in 2003 and 9.0 board feet in 2008 (table 18).

The increase in Oregon lumber recovery since 1968 primarily results from improved sawing technology and characteristics of the Scribner log scale. Technological improvements have made Oregon mills more efficient in numerous ways. Log size (diameter and length) sensing capabilities linked to computers determine the best sawing pattern for logs to recover either the greatest volume or greatest value from each log. Improved sawing accuracy and curve sawing have reduced the amount of size variation in sawn lumber, thus increasing solid wood recovery. Thinner kerf saws reduce the proportion of the log that becomes sawdust. However, inaccuracies inherent in the Scribner log scale could confound recovery estimates, especially because the average log diameter processed by Oregon sawmills has consistently trended downward over the past 50 years as harvesting shifted from old-growth to second-growth forest (Keegan et al. 2006, Keegan et al. 2010b).

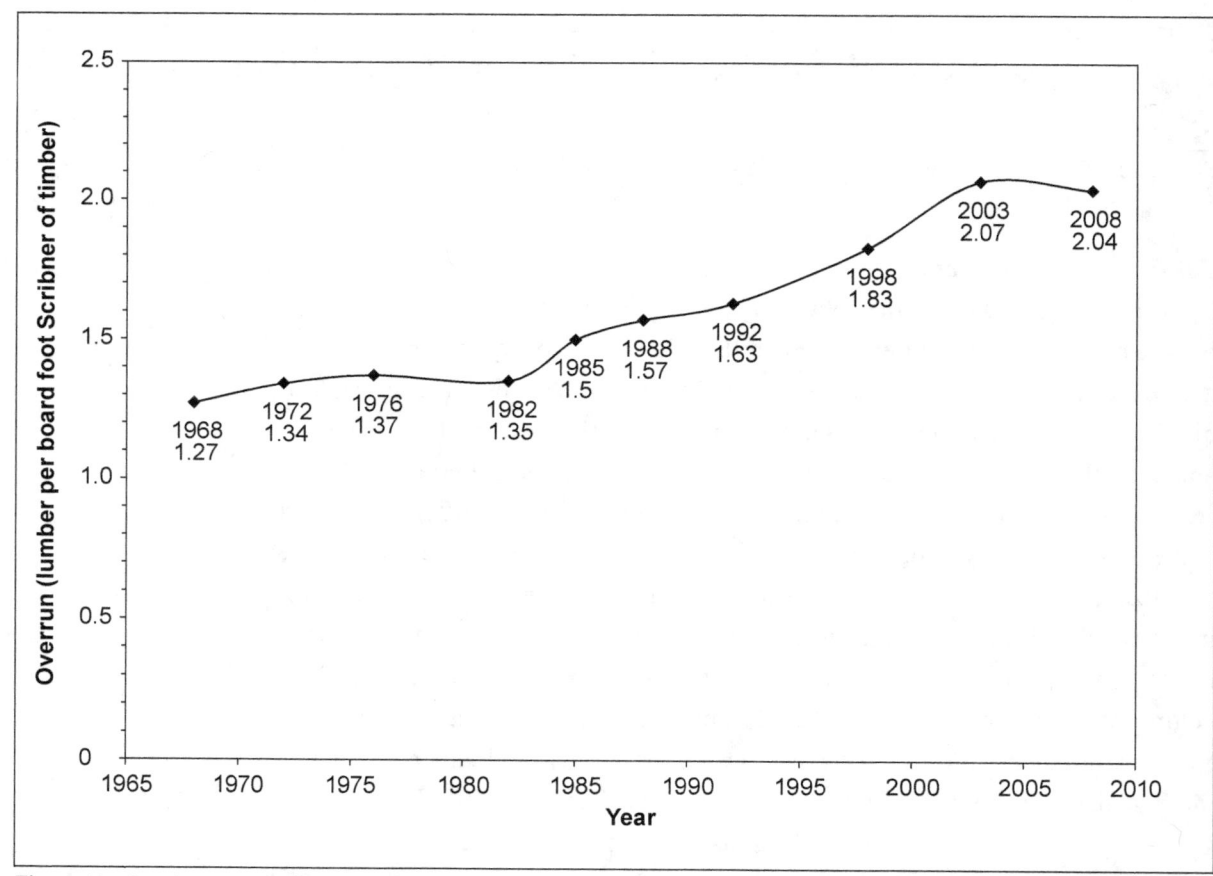

Figure 11—Lumber overrun in Oregon in various years. Source: Brandt et al. 2006; Howard 1984; Howard and Hiserote 1978; Howard and Ward 1991; Manock et al. 1970; Schuldt and Howard 1974; Ward 1995, 2000.

Table 18—Overrun and lumber recovery factor in various years

	1972	1976	1998	2003	2008
Lumber recovery factor	6.95	7.11	8.30	8.64	9.00
Lumber overrun	1.34	1.37	1.83	2.07	2.04

Source: Brandt et al. 2006; Howard 1984; Howard and Hiserote 1978; Howard and Ward 1991, 1998; Manock et al. 1970; Schuldt and Howard 1974; Ward 1995, 1997; Ward et al. 2000.

Log size processed by sawmills—

Despite the long-term trend toward smaller logs discussed above, in 2008, the average log size processed by Oregon sawmills actually increased from 2003 (table 19). Sixty-two percent of logs processed by sawmills had a small-end diameter greater than 10 inches in 2008 versus 54 percent in 2003 (Keegan et al. 2010b). In fact, almost 15 percent of logs processed were greater than 24 inches diameter, rising from 5 percent in 2003.

The increase in log size may be a result of weak lumber markets in 2008. During poor markets, it becomes more difficult for lumber mills to profitably produce lumber from small and low-quality logs. The price of stud grade lumber—which is predominantly made from small logs—fell by a much higher percentage during the recent recession than many other dimension and board and shop lumber grades (Random Lengths 2010b). The reduced use of small-diameter logs, along with reduced incentive to saw lower grades of lumber from marginal-quality logs by sawmills, may have led to the decreased overrun reported in 2008.

> Despite the long-term trend toward smaller logs discussed above, in 2008, the average log size processed by Oregon sawmills actually increased from 2003.

Table 19—Proportion of logs processed by sawmill by small-end diameter

Small-end diameter	2003	2008
< 7 inches	0.14	0.12
7 to 10 inches	0.32	0.26
<10 inches	**0.46**	**0.38**
>10 inches	**0.54**	**0.62**
10 to 24 inches	0.49	0.48
> 24 inches	0.05	0.14

Note: Bold values include totals.

Plywood and Veneer Sector

In Oregon, veneer is used to produce plywood and laminated veneer lumber (LVL). Oregon's plywood and veneer sector produced 2,595 million square feet, 3/8-inch basis (MMSF-3/8-inch) of plywood and 1,428 MMSF-3/8-inch of veneer in 2008, making Oregon the leading producer of plywood in the United States (Adair 2010).

Of the 28 plywood and veneer plants operating in Oregon during 2008, 9 produced veneer only, 11 were both veneer and plywood lay-up operations, and 8 plants produced only plywood (table 20). The number of plywood and veneer facilities has decreased substantially over time. In 1968, there were 138 plywood and veneer plants operating in Oregon (Manock et al. 1970). By 1994, there were just 26 (Ward 1997), and in 1998, there was an increase to 42 mills.

> The number of plywood and veneer facilities has decreased substantially over time.

Table 20—Number of Oregon plywood and veneer mills, selected years 1968–2008

Year	Veneer only	Veneer and plywood	plywood only	All
		Number of mills		
1968	59	58	21	138
1972	46	58	29	133
1976	52	52	28	132
1982	45	37	19	101
1985	36	32	21	89
1988	33	33	21	87
1992	16	13	11	40
1994[a]	—	—	—	26
1998	15	14	13	42
2003	11	13	9	33
2008	9	11	8	28

— = No value in cells.
[a] For 1994, plywood and veneer mills not separated.
Sources: Brandt et al. 2006; Howard 1984; Howard and Hiserote 1978; Howard and Ward 1991, 1988; Manock et al. 1970; Schuldt and Howard 1974; Ward 1995, 1997; Ward et al. 2000.

Oregon's plywood industry grew rapidly between 1954 and 1965 (fig. 12), peaked in the early 1970s, then fluctuated somewhat until the recession in the early 1980s. Production dropped to 5,113 MMSF 3/8-inch in 1982 (Brodie et al. 1978, Warren 1988). Following the recession, plywood production ramped up quickly to 8,381 MMSF-3/8-inch in 1987 then fell rapidly (Adair 2004). By 2008, production had declined to lows not seen since 1954.

Plywood and veneer manufacturers made gains in product recovery from 2003 to 2008. The plywood and veneer recovery factor is the plywood/veneer output (in thousand square feet 3/8-inch basis) divided by the timber input (thousand board feet Scribner). The statewide plywood and veneer recovery factor for Oregon in 2008 was approximately 4.19 square feet per board foot Scribner of log input; in 2003 recovery was 4.0.

The plywood production volume calculated from the 2008 FIDACS census is substantially higher than the plywood production volume published by the Engineered Wood Association (Adair 2010; APA 2009): Oregon plywood production was estimated at 2,595 MMSF 3/8-inch by FIDACS; The American Plywood Association APA reported 2,256 MMSF 3/8-inch total production. The two main reasons for discrepancies in the production numbers are (1) both softwood and hardwood plywood production are included in the FIDACS estimate, whereas APA includes just softwood plywood, and (2) specialty veneer panel products produced by a few Oregon facilities are incorporated in the FIDACS estimate but not in the APA data.

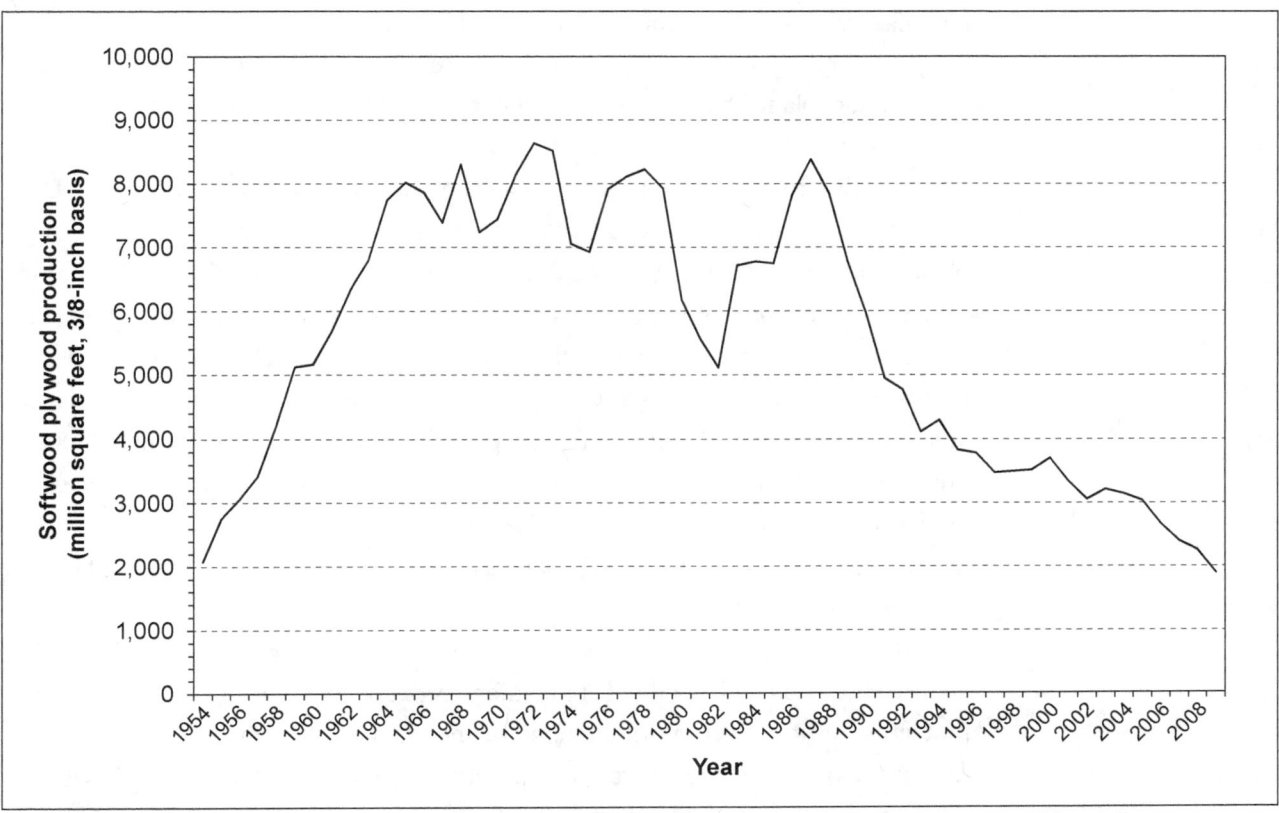

Figure 12—Oregon's softwood plywood production, 1954–2009. Source: Adair 2005, APA 1954–2009, Brodie et al. 1978, Warren 1988.

Pulp and Board Sector

In 2008, 20 pulp and board facilities operated in Oregon; over 85 percent were located in western Oregon. Ten were board plants that produced particleboard, hardboard, and medium-density fiberboard (MDF) and 10 were pulp and paper mills. Board facilities produced a total of 2,001 MMSF of products including particleboard, MDF, and hardboard with a total sales value of close to $404 million. Oregon's pulp and paper sector produced more than 4.4 million dry tons of pulp and paper in 2008 with a sales value close to $2.8 billion, representing a 47 percent increase from sales reported in 2003. China's robust demand for North American pulp and paper has helped drive up demand (Lang 2008). With weaker markets in 2009, pulp and paper sales dropped to approximately $2.5 billion and reconstituted board sales fell to approximately $300 million.

Remaining Sectors

Other primary forest product sectors operating in Oregon during 2008 included both timber- and residue-utilizing manufacturers. Timber-utilizing manufacturers included roundwood pulp-chip conversion operations, export operations; log home manufacturers; cedar product facilities; log furniture manufacturers; and post, small pole, piling, and utility pole facilities. Residue-utilizing sectors included bark product plants, biomass/energy production facilities, and firewood and wood pellet producers.

The eight roundwood pulp-chip conversion facilities produced 374,283 BDUs of clean chips and shavings with a sales value of $44.2 million. Twenty-two log home plants in Oregon in 2008 produced 24,636 thousand lineal feet (MLF) of log products, sold in the form of logs, home kits, or custom-designed homes that generated a total sales value of just under $8 million. The 10 post, small pole, piling, and utility pole plants operating in Oregon during 2008 produced 812,000 pieces with a sales value of $5.2 million. Four log furniture plants operated in Oregon during 2008 and produced 1,040 pieces of log furniture and 26,000 lineal feet of furniture pieces with a combined sales value of just under $860,000. The sales value presented here includes only manufactured products and not the value of logs exported from Oregon.

Of the residue-utilizing sectors, only one commercial biomass/energy operation and two firewood and wood pellet manufacturers operated during 2008. To ensure protection of firm-level information, no further data on these facilities can be released. However, three Oregon bark product facilities produced 37,986 BDUs with a sales value of $9.4 million.

Timber-Processing Capacity: All Sectors

Through the FIDACS census, Oregon mills reported their 8-hour-shift and annual production capacity given sufficient supply and firm product market demand. Each product is reported in different units of volume. Sawmill production capacity was reported in MBF, lumber tally. Veneer production capacity was reported in thousands of square feet (MSF), 3/8-inch basis. Cedar product facilities reported capacity in both hundreds of square feet and MBF. Log home manufacturers measured capacity in MLF; log furniture, post, small pole, and pilings, reported capacity in pieces; and utility pole producers use MLF. Capacity in chipping facilities was reported in BDT. Each of these units was converted to a million board foot Scribner equivalent based on recovery factors appropriate for that sector to estimate the industry's total timber-processing capacity. For example: sawmill production capacity was converted to timber-processing capacity by dividing production capacity in lumber tally by each mill's overrun; veneer capacity was converted by dividing production capacity in square feet of 3/8-inch veneer by each mill's veneer recovery. Capacities for utility pole plants were converted by multiplying capacity in lineal feet by an average Scribner board-foot volume per piece or per lineal foot (Keegan et al. 2006).

Oregon's timber-processing capacity during 2008 was 5.16 billion board feet Scribner (table 21). Sawmills accounted for 3.9 billion board feet (75 percent) of the total timber-processing capacity in the state. Sawmills actually processed just over 2.4 billion board feet of lumber, a utilization rate of 63 percent. The plywood and veneer sectors accounted for 20 percent of statewide capacity; like sawmills, the utilization rate in plywood plants was about 65 percent. Chipping facilities processed 121 MMBF of timber in 2008 but had capacity to produce 176.5 MMBF; their utilization rate of 69 percent was the most of all sectors. These utilization rates suggest that mills in all sectors of solid wood products manufacturing had about one-third of production capacity sitting idle.

Annual timber-processing capacity in Oregon was just over 10 billion board feet Scribner in the 1970s and 1980s, when the state's timber users processed over 7 billion board feet (fig. 13) (Keegan et al. 2006). Following the decline in federal timber offerings, capacity dropped from approximately 10 billion board feet Scribner in 1989 to 4.6 billion in 1996; capacity dropped even during years with high lumber prices (Random Lengths 1976–2010a). Beginning in the late 1990s, with investment in new processing facilities in particular sawmills, and continued relatively high product prices, timber processing capacity increased and reached nearly 5.5 billion board feet before the catastrophic market conditions of late 2008 and 2009. With permanent mill closures in 2009, capacity fell to 4.8 billion board feet Scribner; additional closures followed in 2010 and capacity dropped to 4.5 billion. During the recent poor markets, the portion of capacity used has fallen more dramatically than total capacity, from over 80 percent in the 2003 to 2006 period to 63 percent in 2008 and an estimated 57 percent in 2010.

Oregon's timber-processing capacity during 2008 was 5.16 billion board feet Scribner.

Table 21—Oregon timber-processing capacity and use, 2008

Facility type	Timber processed	Timber-processing capacity[a]	Capacity used
	Million board feet, Scribner		*Percentage*
Sawmills	2,423.6	3,913.3	62
Plywood and veneer	678.0	1,036.3	65
Chipping	121.2	176.5	69
Other facilities[b]	25.3	41.9	60
All facilities	3,248.1	5,168.1	63

[a] Volume of timber reported that could be processed given sufficient supplies of raw materials and firm market demand for products, estimated for each facility by applying the product recovery ratios to production capacity figures provided by each facility.
[b] "Other facilities" includes cedar products, log furniture, log homes, posts, small poles, pilings, and utility poles.

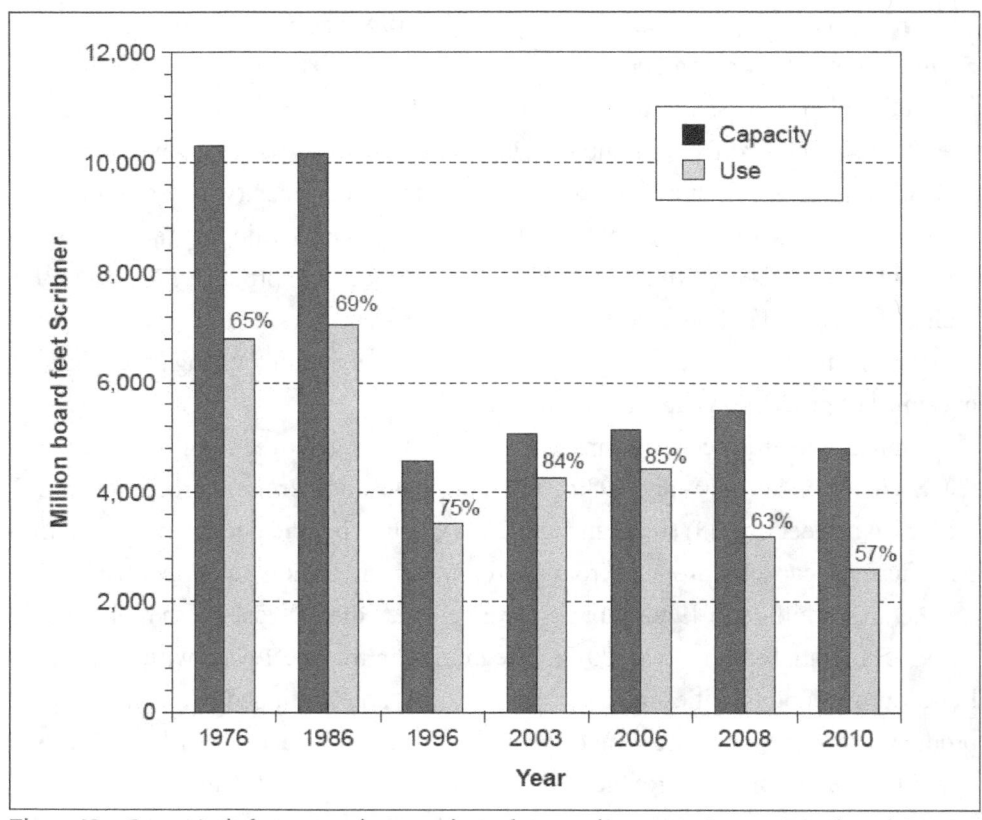

Figure 13—Oregon's timber processing capacity and use, various years. Source: Brandt et al. 2006, Howard 1978, Keegan 2006, Schuldt 1974.

Sawmill Capacity

Because nearly 76 percent of Oregon's total 2008 milling capacity was located in sawmills, this section focuses specifically on the sawmill sector. Oregon's 2008 lumber capacity was approximately 8 billion board feet per year, up modestly from the 7.8 billion reported in 2003 (Brandt et al. 2006). Annual production capacity[8] differed widely among Oregon's 116 sawmills, ranging from under 1 MMBF to more than 400 MMBF per year (table 22). In 2008, 94 percent of lumber production and 93 percent of total lumber-producing capacity was found in the 49 mills with annual capacities greater than 50 MMBF. The 16 mills with capacities of 10 to 50 MMBF accounted for 432 MMBF (5 percent) of total capacity, a 292-MMBF drop from 2003. Mills with annual capacities of 10 MMBF or less, almost half of the sawmills in Oregon, accounted for only 39 MMBF or 0.5 percent of total capacity–down from 2003, when this capacity category accounted for 81 MMBF (1 percent) of total capacity.

> **Oregon's 2008 lumber capacity was approximately 8 billion board feet per year, up modestly from the 7.8 billion reported in 2003.**

---

[8] Production capacity—The volume of product output reported in thousand board feet lumber tally that could be produced given sufficient supplies of raw materials and firm market demand for products. This value was provided by each facility.

Table 22—Active Oregon sawmills, production capacity, and capacity utilization by size class, 2008

Production capacity class	Number of mills	Annual production capacity			Production	Annual production		
		Capacity	Percentage of total capacity	Average capacity per mill		Percentage of total production	Average production per mill	Capacity utilization
		MMBF	*Percent*	*MMBF*	*MMBF*	*Percent*	*MMBF*	*Percent*
Over 100 MMBF annual capacity	29	6,124.5	76.4	211.2	3,444.9	70.4	118.8	56.2
Over 50 to 100 MMBF annual capacity	20	1,424.0	17.8	71.2	1,127.0	22.2	57.2	79.1
Over 10 to 50 MMBF annual capacity	16	431.6	5.4	27.0	345.3	7.1	21.6	80.0
10 MMBF or less annual capacity	51	38.8	0.5	0.8	13.3	0.3	0.3	34.2
Total	116	8,018.9	100	77.5	4,930.5	100	49.5	61.5
120 MBF or greater shift capacity	55	7,751	96.7	140.9	4,728.2	95.9	86.0	61.0
40 MBF to 119.9 MBF shift capacity	9	213.6	2.7	23.7	175.9	3.6	19.5	82.4
Less than 40 MBF shift capacity	52	53.8	0.7	1.0	26.4	0.5	0.5	49.1
Total	116	8,018.9	100	69.1	4,930.5	100	42.5	61.5

MMBF = million board feet lumber tally.
MBF = thousand board feet lumber tally.

In 2008, poor markets drove many of the large mills to sharply curtail production.

Traditionally, the largest mills have operated the greatest number of hours and have had the highest capacity utilization. In 2008, however, poor markets drove many of the large mills to sharply curtail production. Mills in the 10 to 50 MMBF and 50 to 100 MMBF annual capacity categories were still using 80 percent of their capacity while mills with annual capacity of greater than 100 MMBF dropped to 56 percent.

Mill-level detail on annual capacity is not available prior to 2003, but summaries of 8-hour shift capacity are available for several earlier years and offer insights into how mill sizes in Oregon have changed over time (table 23). Censuses of mills in various 8-hour-shift categories and their reported outputs were used in concert with mill directories listing number of shifts operated to estimate annual lumber-processing capacity prior to 2003 (Keegan et al. 2006). During the mid-1950s and again in the late 1980s, annual capacity to produce lumber exceeded 10 billion board feet.

The number of active sawmills in 2003 and 2008 was noticeably greater than previous years almost entirely from gains in mills with small capacity. Part of this increase may be owing to increased efforts to identify active mills for the 2003 and 2008 surveys. The discovery and inclusion of more small mills in the 2003 and 2008 mill surveys could distort previous trends and should be considered when calculating summary metrics such as average output per mill. However, the 58 and 52 mills in this smallest size class accounted for less than 1 percent of Oregon's lumber production and capacity in 2003 and 2008.

Table 23—Active Oregon sawmills by shift capacity, selected years 1958–2008

Year	120 MBF or greater	80 to 119.9 MBF	40 to 79.9 MBF	Less than 40 MBF	All
	Capacity per eight-hour shift				
1958	70	90	157	168	485
1968	59	69	70	102	300
1972	87	60	57	58	262
1976	88	59	45	51	243
1982	71	41	26	23	161
1985	88	35	19	31	173
1988	98	30	11	26	165
1992	56	9	8	13	86[a]
1994	60	9	5	15	89[a]
1998	51	15	6	13	85[a]
2003	57	8	3	58	126
2008	55	5	4	52	116

[a] Includes only mills that participated in the specified survey years.
MBF = thousand board feet.
Sources: Brandt et al. 2006; Howard 1984; Howard and Hiserote 1978; Howard and Ward 1991, 1988; Manock et al. 1970; Schuldt and Howard 1974; Ward 1995, 1997; Ward et al. 2000.

Mill Residue Production and Use

Mill residue from processing timber into primary wood products is the largest source of material for pulp and paper mills, board plants, and other manufacturers of residue-based products as well as fuel for thermal and electrical energy production. They also provide considerable revenue to the mills that generate them. Sawmills and plywood plants processed over 95 percent of the timber used in Oregon and generated over 95 percent of all mill residues. These facilities produced substantially less residue per unit of lumber or plywood manufactured during 2008 than had been reported in previous years.

Mill residue falls into three general categories: (1) coarse residue, including chippable material such as slabs, edging, and trim, log ends, and defective veneer; (2) fine residue, including sawdust, sander dust, and planer shavings; and (3) bark. The volume of mill residue produced during a given year is closely linked to lumber and plywood production in that year. In addition, milling equipment, species and size of logs, amount of defect in logs, and market conditions also influence the amount of residue generated by timber processors.

For 2008, mills reported the volume of residues produced and sold and how those residues were used on a percentage basis. From these percentages, total residue and residue volume factors (mill residue generated per unit of lumber, plywood, or other product produced) were calculated.

Oregon's sawmills and plywood plants produced 4.6 million BDUs of residue, of which only 6.3 thousand BDUs (less than 0.01 percent) was not utilized (table 24). About 69 percent of the residue from Oregon's lumber and plywood facilities was used as raw material by the pulp and paper and reconstituted board industries. The remaining 31 percent of residues was used as fuel (26 percent), other uses such as animal bedding and landscape material (5 percent), and unutilized (less than 1 percent).

> **Mill residue from processing timber into primary wood products is the largest source of material for pulp and paper mills, board plants, and other manufacturers of residue-based products as well as fuel for thermal and electrical energy production.**

Table 24—Production and disposition of wood residues from Oregon's timber processing facilities, 2008

Type of residue	Total utilized	Pulp and board	Fuel	Other uses[a]	Unutilized	Total
			Bone-dry units[b]			
Coarse[c]	2,530,247	2,349,434	158,059	22,754	319	2,530,566
Sawdust	655,974	466,439	183,415	6,121	417	656,390
Planer shavings	371,496	271,404	90,815	9,277	57	371,553
Bark	1,003,899	49,099	761,174	193,626	5,486	1,009,384
All residues	4,561,616	3,136,375	1,193,462	231,779	6,277	4,567,893

[a] "Other uses" primarily include animal bedding, landscape material, and soil additives.
[b] Bone-dry unit = 2,400 pounds of oven-dry wood.
[c] Peeler cores are included in coarse residue.

Residue per thousand board feet of lumber produced dropped from 1.1 BDUs in the early 1970s to approximately 0.7 BDUs in 2008.

Coarse residue was the state's most common wood products residue, comprising 55 percent of all residues. About 93 percent of coarse residue was used in pulp and paper industry and reconstituted board plants, 6 percent was used as fuel, and about 1 percent was sold for other uses. Fines—sawdust and planer shavings together—made up the second largest component (22 percent) of residue, at 1.0 million BDUs in 2008. The vast majority (over 99 percent) of all fines were utilized. Oregon facilities generated 1.0 million BDUs of bark while processing timber, 75 percent of which was used as fuel, most of the remaining 25 percent used for decoration or soil additives.

Residue per thousand board feet of lumber produced dropped from 1.1 BDUs in the early 1970s to approximately 0.7 BDUs in 2008 (table 25). Declining residue factors over time are directly related to gains in mill efficiency; a greater proportion of timber is processed into useable products as efficiency increases. Technologies that have increased mill efficiency include log-size sensing capabilities, curve sawing abilities designed to optimize lumber production from logs with sweep and crook, precision sawing patterns, thinner kerf saw blades, improved edging and trimming, improved chucks to allow veneer logs to be peeled to smaller core diameters, and improved drying techniques (Keegan et al. 2011).

Economic Aspects of Oregon's Forest Products Industry
Forest Products Industry and the Oregon Economy

The forest products industry has long been an important component of the statewide and regional economies in Oregon. This section looks specifically at forest products industry employment and labor income statewide and for multicounty regions and analyzes its contribution to the economy. Because the U.S. government changed the way in which it reported economic data and classified employment by sector in 2001, reliable and consistent data are available only for the recent period

Table 25—Oregon sawmill residue factors: 1972, 1976, 1998, 2003, and 2008

Type of residue	1972	1976	1998	2003	2008
	BDUs per thousand board feet lumber tally[a]				
Coarse[b]	0.45	0.45	0.40	0.37	0.36
Sawdust	0.24	0.22	0.14	0.13	0.11
Planer shavings	0.18	0.17	0.09	0.08	0.08
Bark	0.22	0.20	0.19	0.17	0.16
All residues	1.09	0.84	0.63	0.75	0.71

[a] Bone-dry unit (BDU) = 2,400 pounds of oven-dry wood.
[b] Peeler cores are included in coarse residue.
Note: Years prior to 2008 derived from Brandt et al. 2006; Howard 1984; Howard and Hiserote 1978; Howard and Ward 1991, 1988; Manock et al. 1970; Schuldt and Howard 1974; Ward 1995, 1997; Ward et al. 2000.

2001 to 2009 (USDC BEA 2009). This period formed the basis of the analysis in this section. A few key data points have been estimated for earlier years to provide historical perspective; in particular, for the period since 1990 to capture the dramatic drop in timber availability during the early 1990s.

Employment and labor income data for Oregon and multicounty regions were derived from a number of federal and state data sources:

- Regional Economic Information System Bureau of Economic Analysis, U.S. Department of Commerce (USDC BEA 2009)
- Quarterly Census of Employment and Wages. Bureau of Labor Statistics (U.S. Department of Labor 2011)
- County Business Patterns. Bureau of the Census, U.S. Department of Commerce (USDC CB 2011a)
- Covered Wages and Employment Oregon Labor Market Information System Oregon Employment Department (Oregon Employment Department 2009)

The classification of forest industries used here follows the North American Industrial Classification System (NAICS) available online via the U.S. Department of Commerce (2011b). Specifically, we examined employment in the following forest industries:

- NAICS 113—forestry and logging.
- NAICS 1153—support activities for forestry.
- NAICS 321—wood products manufacturing.
- NAICS 322—paper manufacturing.

These four categories probably understate total employment in the forest products industry (FPI) because they do not include a number of supporting activities. For example, hauling companies, and forest management services performed by government employees, are not included in these categories.

This section focuses on Oregon's primary FPI, which includes logging, processing logs into lumber and other wood products, and processing wood residues from timber-processing plants into outputs such as paper, particleboard, fiberboard, or electricity. The secondary industry includes the further processing of the outputs from the primary manufacturers regardless of the location of the primary manufacturers. The distinction is not always clear, and portions of the secondary industry, such as cutstock manufacturers and portions of the laminated veneer lumber sector, which processes veneer but not timber, are directly linked and highly integrated with the primary industry.

The Oregon FPI employed about 51,000 workers and paid about $3.05 billion (2008 dollars) in labor income in 2008 (fig. 14 and 15). The primary sector accounted for about 70 percent of these employees (35,000 workers), and the

The Oregon FPI employed about 51,000 workers and paid about $3.05 billion (2008 dollars) in labor income in 2008.

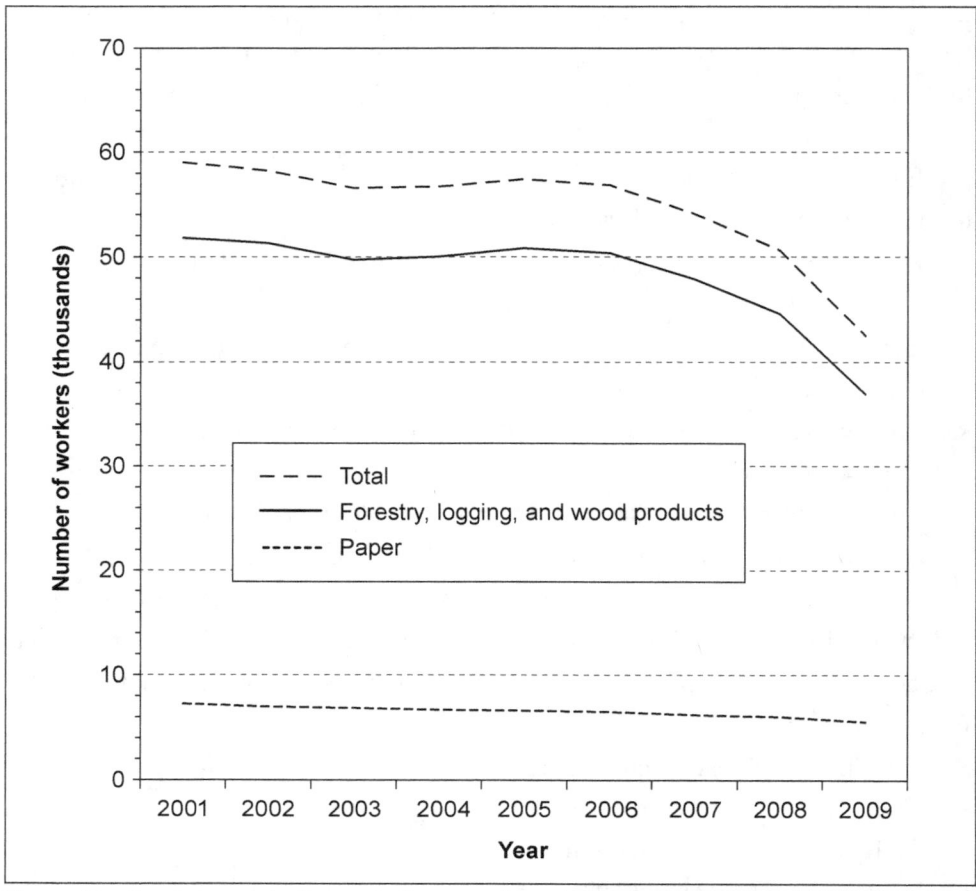

Figure 14—Employment in Oregon's forest products industry, 2001–2009. Source: U.S Bureau of Economic Analysis, Oregon Employment Department 2009.

secondary sector employed the remaining 16,000 workers. Given that a number of workers are excluded from the NAICS categories defining the industry, and because the bulk of wood and paper employment and worker earnings are in the primary sector or in sectors directly linked to it, the analysis focuses on all employment in these categories.

Trends in Forest Products Employment and Labor Income

Many factors influence forest industry employment and labor income. These can be related to the volume, size, and quality of timber; how and where it is harvested and processed; the level of processing; the degree of utilization of wood fiber residue; market conditions; and technological innovations and other factors such as regulations and shifts in forest management regimes/objectives.

Although timber availability was the major factor that shaped Oregon's FPI in the 1990s, market conditions have been the driving force over the past decade. When Oregon's timber harvest fell from 6.9 billion board feet Scribner in 1990 to

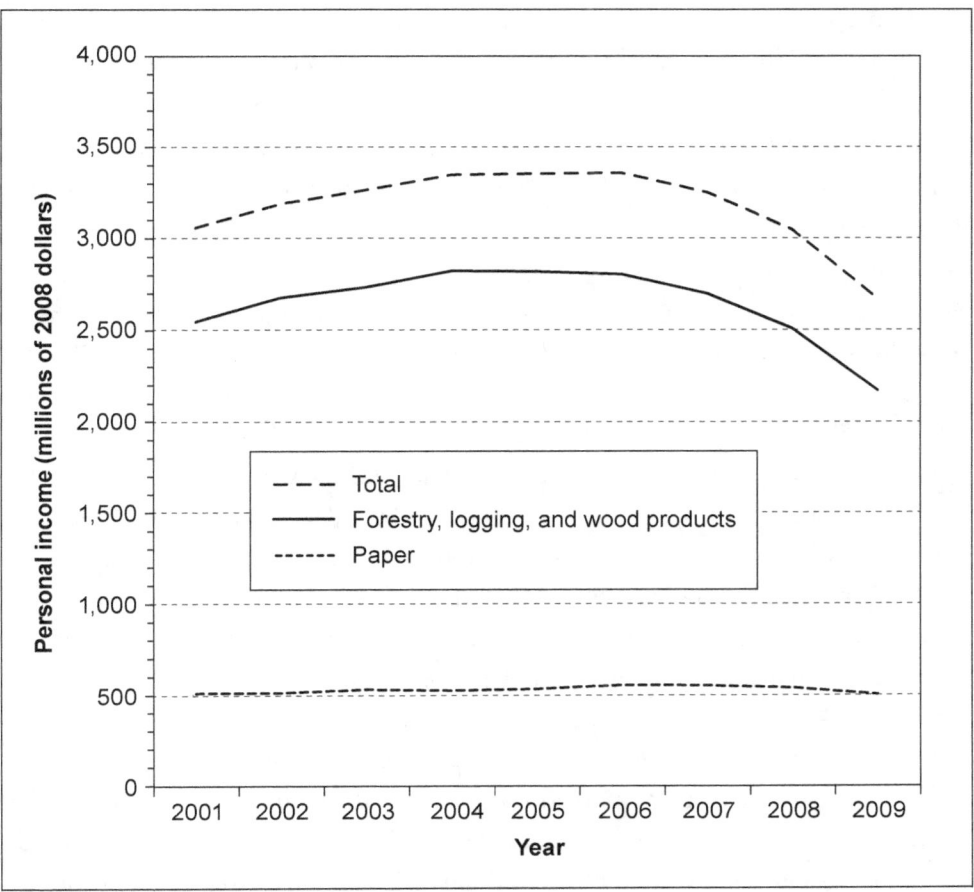

Figure 15—Personal income in Oregon's forest products industry, 2001–2009. Source: U.S Bureau of Economic Analysis, Oregon Employment Department 2009.

3.8 billion board feet in 2000, forest industry employment plummeted from about 72,000 workers in 1990 to just over 58,000 in 1999.

After market conditions improved in the early 2000s, Oregon's wood and paper industry employment actually declined 3 percent from 59,000 workers in 2001 to 57,400 workers in 2005 (U.S. Department of Labor 2011). This reduction resulted from a number of factors, including investment in labor-saving harvesting and wood-processing technology, more efficient use of existing plants and logging equipment, and a shift in log processing from the more labor-intensive plywood and large-log sawmill industry to capital-intensive small log mills. As markets dramatically weakened and harvest and production fell from the peak levels of 2004 and 2005, employment dropped by more than 14,000 workers from 2005 to 2009. Most of the job losses occurred in the logging and wood product sectors.

Labor income includes wages and salaries and selected employer-paid benefits (such as retirement). Because mill managers can adjust labor more easily than other factors of production (by changing workers' hours, for example), labor income is

Labor income fell by more than 30 percent between 2005 and 2009 as markets softened and the recessionary conditions intensified.

more closely correlated with output than employment. Also, labor income provides a consistent measure of economic activity at different scales; values can be scaled up for statewide estimates and scaled down for county-level estimates.

Figure 15 shows that, after adjusting for inflation, there was 10-percent growth in labor income from 2001 to 2005. Although the number of forest industry workers decreased by about 3 percent over that period, earnings per worker increased by more than 25 percent. This period of rising wages was short lived; labor income fell by more than 30 percent between 2005 and 2009 as markets softened and the recessionary conditions intensified (OED 2009, USDC BEA 2009).

The Forest Products Industry and Oregon's Economic Base

Economic base is a term used to describe and analyze the major industries providing jobs within a given market area. Activities are divided into two categories, basic and non-basic. Basic industries are those exporting from the area and bringing in wealth from outside; non-basic industries support basic industries. Thus, Oregon's economic base consists of the industries that sell their products outside the state or are otherwise injecting new funds into the state's economy. These new dollars are spent and re-spent within Oregon, creating additional jobs and incomes; this phenomenon is called the multiplier effect. Most long-run and short-run trends in the overall economy are consequences of events in the basic industries. The designation of an industry or industry component as basic or derivative can vary by region and over time. In some areas, certain service industries, as well as some construction activity, may also be basic activities. But estimating the basic and derivative components of the construction and service industries is complex and imprecise, and may change substantially from year to year. Similarly, other components of income (such as unearned income) contain both basic and derivative components and they are also difficult to measure. Refereed research publications conclude that basic industries provide the single best statistical explanation of state economic trends (Polzin 1990, 2000; Polzin et al. 1988).

Oregon's economic base consists of the FPI, agriculture, fishing, other manufacturing (nonforest products), transportation (rail, truck, water, and associated port activities), tourism, and the federal government (both civilian and military). Labor income rather than employment was used to analyze Oregon's economic base. There are significant differences between average wages per worker in the various basic industries. For example, the average wage per worker in certain manufacturing industries is more than $100,000 while the corresponding figure for hotel/motel workers is about $19,000. Labor income has been converted to 2008 dollars to correct for inflation.

The largest component of Oregon's economic base in 2008 was nonforest products manufacturing, which accounted for about 52 percent of basic labor income. The FPI represented approximately 14 percent of the state's economic base. Agriculture and fishing, tourism and transportation (rail, truck, water and the ports) each accounted for about 5 to 7 percent of the economic base.

The FPI's share of Oregon's economic base declined from approximately 16 percent in 2001 to roughly 14 percent in 2008. Taking a longer view (and recognizing the difficulties associated with estimating a figure derived under a different statistical reporting system), the FPI accounted for approximately 23 percent of basic labor income in 1990. Therefore, the share of Oregon's economic base represented by the FPI has declined by about 9 percentage points between 1990 and 2008. This decline is especially troubling for Oregon's rural areas, where the forest industry has played an important role in rural employment for decades and few other skilled labor jobs are available.

The share of Oregon's economic base represented by the forest products industry has declined by about 9 percentage points between 1990 and 2008.

Regional Dependence on the Forest Products Industry

Although the statewide share of labor income from forest industries decreased from 2003 to 2008, the ranking of forest industry dependence by resource area remained the same. Regional dependence on forest industries was determined by calculating forest-sector labor income as a percentage of total labor income in each Oregon county. County-level values were then aggregated into the four resource areas described previously.

Counties in the Southwest Resource Area were the most dependent; less than 6 percent of labor income was attributable to forest industries. Within that region, Curry and Douglas Counties were the most dependent; forest industries comprised 17 and 13 percent of their economic base, respectively (fig. 16). In the Central Resource Area, forest industries generated 4.7 percent of labor income. Three counties were the most dependent: Crook, Jefferson, and Lake Counties. In the Blue Mountains Resource Area, forest industries totaled 3 percent of labor income overall and contributed to 14 percent of Grant County's economic base. Finally, forest industries in the Northwest Resource Area overall provided only 2 percent of total labor income. The economic base in this area is largely dominated by the Portland metropolitan area. However, in Clatsop County, over one-fourth (27 percent) of labor income came from forest industries, making it the most forest-dependent county in the state with respect to economic base. This local dependence was masked when labor income was aggregated to the regional level.

Figure 17 depicts forest dependency in a different way. Labor income from forest industries in each county was divided by the total statewide labor income from forest industries. These percentages were then ranked and placed into the five

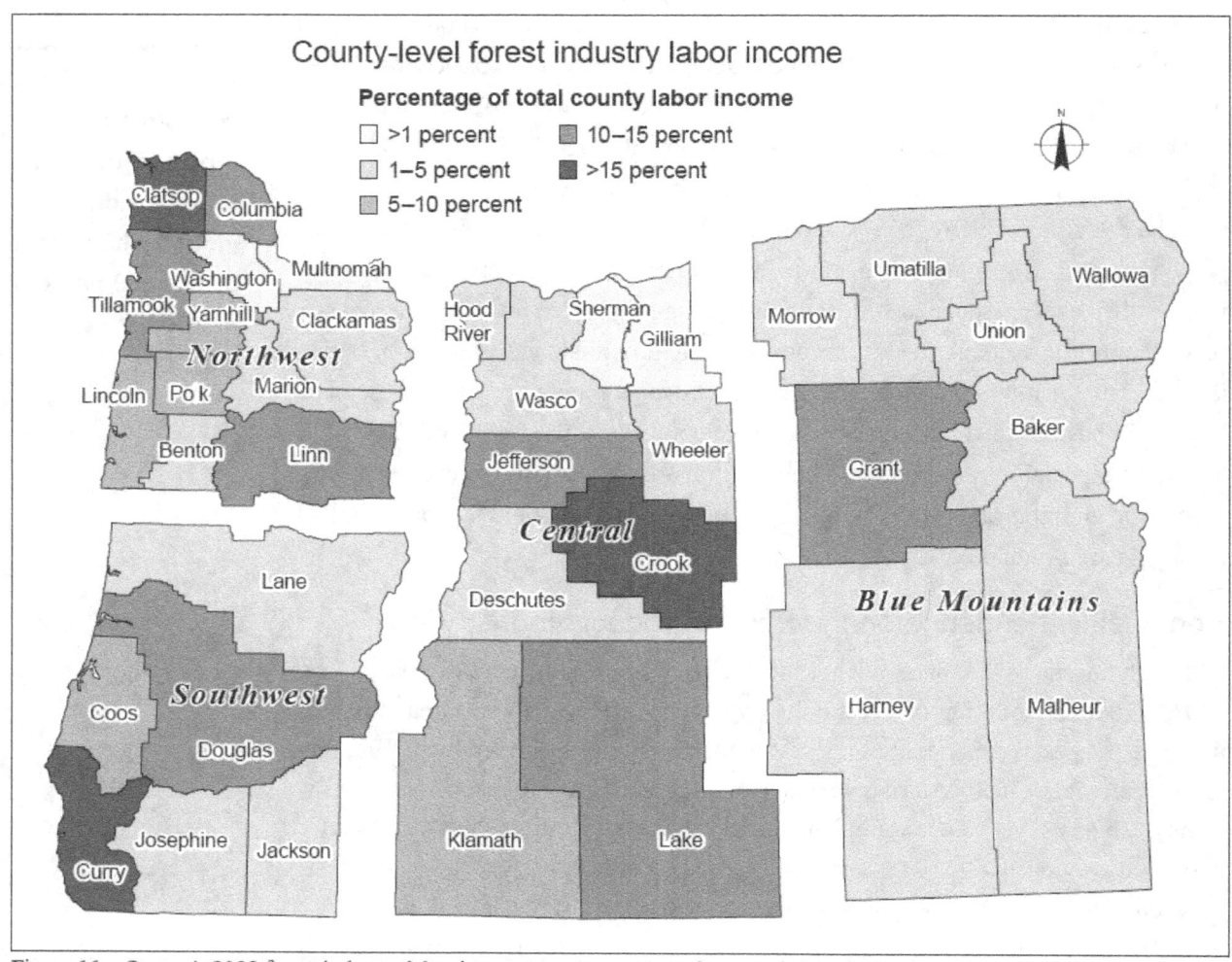

Figure 16—Oregon's 2008 forest industry labor income as a percentage of economic base by county.

Although the Southwest Resource Area was the most forest-dependent in terms of economic base, as a percentage of total statewide forest industry labor income, the Northwest Resource Area is the most dependent.

categories displayed on the map. Although the Southwest Resource Area was the most forest-dependent in terms of economic base, as a percentage of total statewide forest industry labor income, the Northwest Resource Area is the most dependent. Manufacturers in the Northwest Resource Area generated 55 percent of total FPI labor income in 2008. Forest industries in the Southwest Resource Area contributed 32 percent, Central Resource Area 10 percent, and Blue Mountains Resource Area 3 percent of wood products income. In total, the North and Southwest Resource Areas, combined, contributed 87 percent of the total FPI labor income in the state.

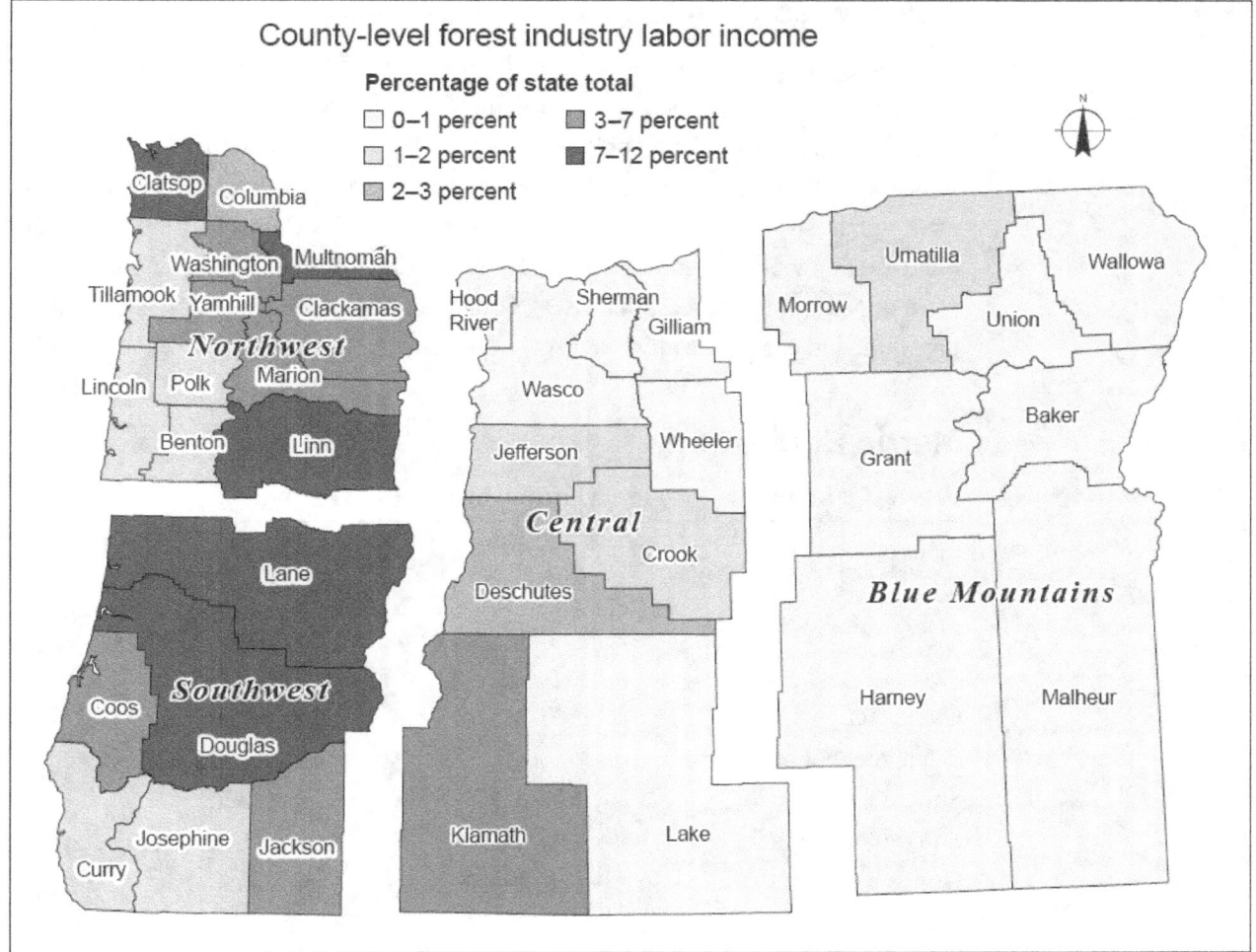

Figure 17—Oregon's 2008 forest industry labor income by county as a percentage of total state forest industry labor income.

Forest industries in Lane County in the Southwest Resource Area generated over $350 million in labor income in 2008, the highest in the state. Douglas and Curry County combined had over 25 percent of the statewide FPI income while the other counties had between 10 and 20 percent. Clatsop County in the Northwest Resource Area is the only county to have the highest dependency rating in both figures 16 and 17. This suggests that Clatsop County may be a county of concern whose economy could be heavily affected by market conditions and policies affecting forest sector employment.

Acknowledgments

In the second series of Oregon's Forest Industries Data Collection System, we express thanks to the people who shared their information with us and gave their time and comments to help publish this report. Special thanks to participating industry, mill owners, and facility representatives; Gary Lettman, Oregon Department of Forestry; Linc Cannon, Oregon Forest Industries Council; Eric Hansen and Scott Leavengood, Oregon State University; Dorian Smith, Washington Department of Natural Resources; the USDA Forest Service Forest Inventory and Analysis program; and especially all reviewers.

Metric Equivalents

When you know:	Multiply by:	To find:
Inches	2.54	Centimeters
Feet	0.3048	Meters
Miles	1.609	Kilometers
Acres	0.405	Hectares
Cubic feet	0.0283	Cubic meters
Cubic feet per acre	0.06997	Cubic meters per hectare
Square feet	0.0929	Square meters
Square feet per acre	0.229	Square meters per hectare
Ounce	28349.5	Milligrams
Pounds	0.453	Kilograms
Pounds per cubic foot	16.018	Kilograms per cubic meter
Tons per acre	2.24	Megagrams per hectare
Degrees Fahrenheit	$(°F - 32)/1.8$	Degrees Celsius

References

Adair, C. 2004. Regional production and market outlook: structural panels and engineered wood products 2004–2009. Report E170. Tacoma, WA: APA—The Engineered Wood Association. 56 p.

Adair, C. 2010. Structural panel and engineered wood yearbook. APA Economics Report E176. Tacoma, WA: APA—The Engineered Wood Association. 56 p.

American Plywood Association [APA]. 2009–2010. Member directory. http://www.apawood.org/membermills/startsearch.cfm. (June 2011).

Andrews, A., Kutara, K. 2005. Oregon's timber harvests: 1849–2004. Salem, OR: Oregon Department of Forestry. 154 p.

Brandt, J.P.; Morgan, T.A.; Dillon, T.; Lettman, G.J.; Keegan, C.E. lll.; Azuma, D.L. 2006. Oregon's forest products industry and timber harvest, 2003. Gen. Tech. Rep. PNW-GTR-681. Portland, OR: U.S. Department of Agriculture, Forest Service, Pacific Northwest Research Station. 53 p.

Brodie, D.J.; McMahon, R.O.; Gabelis, W.H. 1978. Oregon's forest resources: their contributions in the state's economy. Res. Bull. 23. Corvallis, OR: Oregon State University Forest Research Laboratory. 80 p.

Connaughton, K.P.; Polzin, P.E.; Schallau, C.H. 1985. Tests of the economic base model of growth for a timber dependent region. Forest Science. 31(3): 717–725.

Donnegan, J.; Campbell, S.; Azuma, D., tech. eds. 2008. Oregon's forest resources, 2001–2005: five-year Forest Inventory and Analysis report. Gen. Tech. Rep. PNW-GTR-765. Portland, OR: U.S. Department of Agriculture, Forest Service, Pacific Northwest Research Station. 186 p.

Ehinger, P.F. 2009. Forest industry data: Oregon, Washington, Idaho, Montana, and California. Operating mills and other data. Consulting Forester, Paul F. Ehinger & Associates, 2300 Oakmont Way, No. 212, Eugene, OR 97401.

Ehinger, P.F. 2011. Personal communication. Consulting forester, Paul F. Ehinger & Associates, 2300 Oakmont Way, No. 212, Eugene, OR 97401.

Gebert, K.M.; Keegan, C.E., III.; Willits, S.; Chase, A. 2002. Utilization of Oregon's timber harvest and associated direct economic effects, 1998. Gen. Tech. Rep. PNW-GTR-532. Portland, OR: U.S. Department of Agriculture, Forest Service, Pacific Northwest Forest and Range Experiment Station. 16 p.

Howard, J.O. 1984. Oregon's forest products industry: 1982. Resour. Bull. PNW-RB-118. Portland, OR: U.S. Department of Agriculture, Forest Service, Pacific Northwest Forest and Range Experiment Station. 79 p.

Howard, J.O.; Hiserote, B.A. 1978. Oregon's forest products industry: 1976. Resour. Bull. PNW-RB-79. Portland, OR: U.S. Department of Agriculture, Forest Service, Pacific Northwest Forest and Range Experiment Station. 102 p.

Howard, J.O.; Ward, F.R. 1988. Oregon's forest products industry: 1985. Resour. Bull. PNW-RB-149. Portland, OR: U.S. Department of Agriculture, Forest Service, Pacific Northwest Research Station. 90 p.

Howard, J.O.; Ward, F.R. 1991. Oregon's forest products industry: 1988. Resour. Bull PNW-RB-183. Portland, OR: U.S. Department of Agriculture, Forest Service, Pacific Northwest Research Station. 91 p.

Keegan, C.E., III; Morgan, T.A.; Blatner, K.A.; Daniels, J.M. 2010a. Trends in lumber processing in the western United States. Part I: Board foot Scribner volume per cubic foot of timber. Forest Products Journal. 60(2): 133–139.

Keegan, C.E., III; Morgan, T.A.; Blatner, K.A.; Daniels, J.M. 2010b. Trends in lumber processing in the western United States. Part II: Overrun and lumber recovery factors. Forest Products Journal. 60(2): 140–143.

Keegan, C.E., III; Morgan, T.A.; Blatner, K.A.; Daniels, J.M. [N.d.]. Trends in lumber processing in the western United States. Part III: Residue recovered vs. lumber produced. Manuscript in preparation.

Keegan, C.E., lll; Morgan, T.A.; Gebert, K.M.; Brandt, J.P.; Blatner , K.A.; Spoelma, T.P. 2006. Timber-processing capacity and capabilities in the Western United States. Journal of Forestry. 104(5): 262–268.

Lang, C. 2008. Lacking raw material. Pulp Mill Watch Factsheet. http://www.pulpmillwatch.org/countries/china/. (June 2011).

Lockwood-Post. 2008. Directory of pulp and paper mills. The Americas, Traveler's Edition. Atlanta, GA: RISI. 515 p.

Manock, E.R.; Choate, G.A.; Gedney, D.R. 1970. Oregon timber industries: wood consumption and mill characteristics, 1968. Salem, OR: Oregon Department of Forestry. 122 p.

Miller, H.M. 1982. Forest, people and Oregon: a history of forestry in Oregon. Salem, OR: Oregon State University Department of Forestry. 52 p.

National Bureau of Economic Research [NBER]. 2010. Business Cycle Dating Committee. http://www.nber.org/cycles/sept2010.html. (May 2011).

Oregon Employment Department [OED]. 2009. Covered employment and wages. http://www.qualityinfo.org/olmisj/CEP?indtype=N&areacode=01000000&action=industry&submit2=Continue. (February 23, 2011).

Oregon Department of Forestry [ODF]. 2010. Quarterly adjusted softwood log price index. http://www.oregon.gov/odf/resource_planning/docs/logpricegraph.xls. (February 2011).

Oregon Department of Forestry [ODF]. 2011. Complete harvest data 1986–present. http://www.oregon.gov/ODF/STATE_FORESTS/FRP/annual_reports.shtml. (February 2011).

Polzin, P.E. 1990. The verification process and regional science. The Annals of Regional Science. 24: 61–67.

Polzin, P.E. 2000. Why some states grow faster than others: new growth models for state economic policy. Growth and Change. 32: 413–415.

Polzin, P.E.; Connaughton, K.; Schallau, C. H.; and Sylvester, J.T. 1988. Forecasting accuracy and structural stability of the economic base model. The Review of Regional Studies. 18: 23–36.

Random Lengths. 1976–2010a. Random Lengths yearbook: forest product market prices and statistics. Eugene, OR: Random Length Publications, Inc.

Random Lengths. 2007–2010b. Big book: the buyers and sellers directory of the forest products industry. Eugene, OR: Random Lengths Publications, Inc.

Random Lengths. 2007–2011. Yardstick. [Newsletter]. http://www.randomlengths. com/base.asp?s1=Newsletters&s2=Yardstick. (June 2011).

Schuldt, J.P.; Howard, J.O. 1974. Oregon forest industries: wood consumption and mill characteristics, 1972. Spec. Rep. 427. Corvallis, OR: Oregon State University. 113 p.

The Engineered Wood Association. 2009. Regional production and market outlook, U.S, structural panel production by state, 2009. Tacoma, WA: APA—The Engineered Wood Association. 8 p.

U.S. Department of Agriculture, Forest Service [USDA FS]. 2011. Forest Inventory and Analysis EVALIDator Version 1.5.00. Arlington, VA. http://apps.fs.fed.us/Evalidator/tmattribute.jsp and Forest Inventory Data Online (FIDO) http://199.128.173.26/fido/index.html. (July 2011).

U.S. Department of Agriculture, Forest Service [USDA FS]. 2006. Forest Inventory and Analysis glossary. On file with: Forestry Sciences Laboratory, 620 SW Main Street, Suite 400, Portland, OR, 97205.

U.S. Department of Agriculture, Forest Service [USDA FS]. 2012. Forest products sold and harvested from national forests and grasslands. http://www. fs.fed.us/forestmanagement/products/sold-harvest/index.shtml/index.shtml. (March 13, 2012).

U.S. Department of Commerce, Bureau of Economic Analysis [USDC BEA]. 2009. State annual personal income. http://www.bea.gov/regional/spi/default.cfm ?selTable=SA25N&selSeries=NAICS. (February 2011).

U.S. Department of Commerce, Census Bureau [USDC CB]. 2009. Annual survey of manufacturers. http://factfinder2.census.gov/faces/nav/jsf/pages/ index.xhtml. (June 2011).

U.S. Department of Commerce, Census Bureau [USDC CB]. 2011a. County business patterns. http://censtats.census.gov/cbpnaic/cbpnaic.shtml. (July 2011).

U.S. Department of Commerce, Census Bureau [USDC CB]. 2011b. North American Industry Classification System (NAICS). http://www.census.gov/eos/ www/naics/. (June 2011).

U.S. Department of Labor. 2011. Bureau of Labor Statistics. http://www.bls.gov/. (June 2011).

U.S. Office of Management and Budget. 1997. North American industry classification system (NAICS). Lanham, MD: Bernan Press: 1247 p.

Ward, F.R. 1995. Oregon's forest products industry: 1992. Resour. Bull. PNW-RB-207. Portland, OR: U.S. Department of Agriculture, Forest Service, Pacific Northwest Research Station. 89 p.

Ward, F.R. 1997. Oregon's forest products industry: 1994. Resour. Bull. PNW-RB-216. Portland, OR: U.S. Department of Agriculture, Forest Service, Pacific Northwest Research Station. 70 p.

Ward, F.R.; Lettman G.J.; Hiserote, B.A. 2000. Oregon's forest products industry: 1998. Portland, OR: U.S. Department of Agriculture, Forest Service, Pacific Northwest Research Station. Oregon Department of Forestry. 82 p.

Warren, D.D. various years. Production, prices, employment, and trade in Northwest forest industries. Portland, OR: U.S. Department of Agriculture, Forest Service, Pacific Northwest Research Station.

Washington Department of Natural Resources. 2010. Washington mill survey 2008. Series report #20. Olympia, WA: 98 p. http://www.dnr.wa.gov/publications/obe_rpt_millsurv_2008.pdf. (April 2011).

Western Wood Products Association [WWPA]. 2010. 1964–2009. Statistical yearbook of the Western lumber industry. Portland, OR.